THE ETHICAL ROADMAP

COMPLIANCE PROFESSIONALS CAN LEARN HOW TO EXAMINE, BENCHMARK, AND CONSTANTLY IMPROVE THEIR OWN ORGANIZATIONS.

DR. AMIT DAS

To

All my bosses who made a difference in my professional career.

Contents

Foreword

This book, "*The Ethical Roadmap*" contains a combination of ideas, views, perceptions, and practises in various business operations. It is an essential book that is easy to read and contains several quotations and examples of various business tasks. Based on research findings, it delves further into reality. This book uses a flexible modular approach to shed light on modern corporate challenges by providing a full description of the corporate governance process and the many motivations within today's governance system, as well as prospective solutions in context. This book provides clear, detailed, and practical information for practitioners and decision-makers in any organization or corporation. It describes in layman's words the skills, tools, and attitude required to build and deliver a best-practice compliance and ethics program—one that complies with legal, stakeholder, and societal standards and protects your company from fines, penalties, and reputational harm.

This book provides cutting-edge material, including innovative and unusual study aids as well as fresh, thought-provoking content, with an emphasis on integrating corporate governance into practical management.

The authors' contribution to sensitizing diverse stakeholders of contemporary organizations on corporate governance, corporate social responsibility, and business ethics in general. The book *"The Ethical Roadmap"* also attempts to help company managers improve their ethical awareness and decision-making abilities, as well as address their issues. This book is intended not just for management students, but also as a resource for academics and professionals in the area.

The *"The Ethical Roadmap"* provides readers with a thorough overview of business ethics and corporate governance ideas. The necessity of ethical principles in addressing ethical challenges in today's highly dynamic corporate environment is emphasized in this book. It also goes into the corporate governance structure in great depth. Its components, as well as how it is implemented in India and overseas, numerous real-life examples offered in this book aid in the learning of ideas, and discussions centred on these instances provide a deeper grasp of real-world business procedures. This book *"The Ethical Roadmap"* is the most reader-friendly text on the market since it takes a complete, realistic, inventive, and practical approach to the topic. This book covers a wide range of business ethics ideas and emphasises the role of ethical principles in resolving moral difficulties in the workplace. The author connects the multiple leyers of human behaviour to business compliance in his work, illustrating how all three may be used together to create a holistic learning environment. Dr. Amit Das brings out tiny but significant successes in reimagining a current compliance training program or building new courses across fully compliant platforms, which may transform sceptics into champions of learning. The book discusses how to engage employees in a way that inspires them while avoiding sanctions and reputational damage. The human component may be disregarded while formulating laws and regulations. However, an effective compliance and ethical program relies heavily on the human component. It's not just about selecting people who will follow orders but also about engaging with them so that they will advocate business ideals.

In addition to business realities, the author offers a critical perspective on how these things can only be accomplished by harmonising culture, strategy, compliance processes, and other perks like remuneration. The misconception that governance, risk management, and compliance are minor considerations in the inner workings of a company is refuted. In reality, it is the success of these efforts that contributes to total market gains, with the high-profile failures of huge banking institutions, large oil firms, and real estate used to demonstrate the point. This book helps readers improve their reasoning and analytical abilities needed to apply ethical notions to business by using a wide variety of India-centric examples. This book is highly relevant for students and professionals today due to its coverage of the ethical theories underlying business and their application in the real world, as well as a special focus on ethical issues in consumer protection and the information technology sector, whistle-blowing, and real-life corporate incidents. This book is a thorough foundation for comprehending the most pressing global business concerns, including business sustainability, corporate governance, and organizational ethics, is available as an e-book.

This book's entertaining tone will take its readers beyond the word "compliance," which is perceived as so negative by many, and illustrate how to win hearts and minds. Telling tales is a practical and beneficial technique to make learning more memorable and effective. The author deserve praise for his innovative approach to providing a must-read for every professional and student. For those teaching business ethics at universities and business schools, this is a foundational management text.

In examining what works and what doesn't, the book strikes the correct balance between ethics and values on the one hand and compliance program aspects on the other. It is well-written and easy to comprehend, and it offers useful information for both seasoned compliance professionals and newbies to the industry. It deftly incorporates real-world tales and anecdotes into the lessons in a fun way, bringing the debate to life. It is required reading for anyone on the compliance path and is destined to become a compliance literature classic. The author, Dr. Amit Das, gives the depth of knowledge required to assist organizations in navigating ethics and compliance in an effective and integrated manner. *"The Ethical Roadmap"* investigates why rules-based, tick-box, defended compliance continues to fail, and proposes a new strategy for businesses that want to thrive and prosper. The author of this book has succeeded in expressing what everyone should know and do in terms of compliance and ethics in a precise, pleasant, and readily accessible manner. The author should be complimented for his approach to producing a book that every professional should read. This book addresses a vacuum in the literature on business ethics by using an overall interdisciplinary approach and merging new research results from fields like economics, business administration, behavioural economics, philosophy, psychology, and sociology. The book opens with a definition of business ethics, a description of its goals, and a discussion of the relevance of business ethics to companies, the economy, and society. This is a thorough and practical handbook that will assist you in dealing with real-life ethical difficulties that arise in the workplace. It will guide you through the process of honing the critical thinking and analytical abilities you'll need to tackle the particular set of issues that arise when ethics and commerce intersect. This book explains the philosophical foundations of business ethics and interprets this theory in practical terms, highlighting the moral consequences of managerial actions. This version includes new information on global ethics, the financial crisis, and ethical sustainability. Learning goals at the beginning of each chapter, which give a roadmap to what is taught and how to utilise it, are among the new, student-friendly elements.

The best practises described in the chapter are summarised in *"The Ethical Roadmap,"* which allows students and professionals to examine, benchmark, and constantly improve their own organization. This book gives the tools and concepts needed to comprehend and effectively handle ethical dilemmas wherever you are in the world, thanks to a genuinely worldwide viewpoint and a variety of creative learning features. To get a better grasp of markets, business, and economic life, this book presents a study of ethics and values.

Preface

" Ethics is knowing the difference between what you have a right to do and what is right to do"- Potter Stewart

Ethics extends beyond the realm of business. In the long term, ethical business and marketing methods are sustainable. Corporate business processes must be constantly improved, transparent, compassionate, truthful, and respectful. Such businesses set the bar for good corporate governance. Corporate corruption tales abound in today's news. These incidents are frequently blamed on top-level decision-makers, and properly so in most situations. Modern business executives are responsible for both promoting ethical conduct and dealing with ethical snafus that arise during their term. The author of *"The Ethical Roadmap"* will discuss major ethical issues in this book. Author will leverage his 20 years of experience as a leader in many industries to help you fine-tune your ethical framework. You have a responsibility to fulfil. That assumption is that you would conduct yourself in an ethical manner and represent your company as such. As a result, this is a very crucial discussion that you should have. And the author wants to offer a set of principles and things to think about in your debate so that you can go through that grey area with the best chance of coming up with a good, sound ethical solution.

People are where ethics may be found. In truth, the organization's ethics are represented by its leaders. The majority of businesses have a set of codified ethical guidelines. And although that gives advice, which is wonderful, whatever conduct emanates from the organization's executives symbolises the organization's ethics. As a result, the leaders are the organization's ethics. Whether you like it or not, you're representing a organization. In the current corporate environment, ethics in business is a new dimension that has evolved internationally. Transparency, responsibility, and accountability not only increase consumer confidence but also raise employee morale. Organizations throughout the world are still being harmed and brought down by systematic noncompliance or the sins of a few, and the media are full of stories about corporate scandals and crimes. This is despite growing ethical expectations from stakeholders, the ability of social media to expose businesses, the proliferation of compliance rules and regulations, and the growing number of policies, processes, and compliance officers put in place in response. So, why is it that compliance isn't working? In examining what works and what doesn't, the book strikes the correct balance between ethics and values on the one hand and compliance programme aspects on the other. It is well-written and easy to comprehend, and it offers useful information for both seasoned compliance professionals and newbies to the industry. It deftly incorporates real-world tales and anecdotes into the lessons in a fun way, bringing the debate to life. It is required reading for anyone on the compliance path.

This is a book for everyone who wants to learn how to increase employee engagement and motivation. *"The Ethical Roadmap"* highlights the benefits that a really effective compliance and ethics programme can provide when it works hand in hand with a values-based culture of shared ownership, including competitive advantage, career fulfilment, employee and customer loyalty, and brand improvement. Fully Complaint argues that the best compliance training programmes must be both practical and adaptable in order to modify employee behaviour and, as a result, reduce the likelihood of misbehaviour occurring in the first place. Only by balancing the demands of the employees with those of the company can compliance training be successful. In this instructive read, Dr. Amit Das challenges typical compliance training programmes in a number of thought-provoking ways. With a seemingly never-ending list of compliance concerns to handle, Dr. Amit Das believes that businesses should select learning programs that serve higher and broader goals, with the ultimate objective of fostering a resilient workplace culture that prioritises integrity and ethics.

Employees and decision-makers need clear, detailed, and practical compliance information to help their companies prosper and thrive. Compliance and ethics are sometimes viewed as stringent sets of rules and procedures, making individuals fearful of deviating from the norm rather than fostering buy-in. This book questions this industry standard, portraying it as the reason why compliance is a faulty idea in business. It is beneficial because it paves the way for clear documentation and defensible measures for businesses that want to avoid any potential legal liabilities brought on by their personnel. Focusing on the what and how without addressing why leads to an emotional connection and disengaged employees who are more likely to burn out. Employees who are engaged are more inclined to be proud and ardent about supporting the corporate principles with which they agree. In summary, an optimistic attitude yields greater results than a fear-based strategy. A compliance and ethics program, when effectively implemented, transforms employees into stakeholders. An organization's culture of shared ownership can be transformed by this values-based culture. It's not only about spreading good vibes. Compliance and ethics are great ways to set clear standards for workers and make it easier for them to understand how success is assessed. Providing honest, non-confrontational feedback to decision-makers in order to help staff thrive.Making Ethical Decisions uses the weight-of-reasons method throughout the text to educate students on how to handle ethical dilemmas they may face. The goal of this decision-making framework is to solve ethical quandaries rather than to faithfully apply certain philosophical perspectives on what is good. Using this technique, the author stresses the need for employees at all levels to carefully consider the ethical consequences of their activities, and it may be implemented at the individual, organizational, and stakeholder levels. Each chapter includes a case that walks students through the framework's application, as well as mini-cases that allow students to experiment with the framework on their own.

Clear expectations channelled toward good progress transform feedback into something to be desired rather than feared. This book lays the groundwork for this strategy. Rules can help establish expectations, but it's the culture of the organization that makes it effective. *"The Ethical Roadmap"* recognizes the delicate balance that must be achieved and offers a clear method to do so.

Dr. Amit Das believes that risk management should not be centred on what has occurred or the issues that need to be addressed. Instead, concentrate on prospective difficulties and how to be proactive when it comes to risk management. He reminds the reader that senior management's actions are significantly more important in shaping organizational culture. He explains how senior leaders may achieve their objectives by incorporating the proper organization, processes, and technology. And how effective CEOs and directors shape, manage, and monitor their organizations in order to achieve these goals. This book will assist you in comprehending the crucial architecture that underpins every organization's driving power. You'll discover how to avoid key errors by reading this book, as well as how to seize the proper opportunities for continuing company success. The book investigates why some great corporations have failed while others have thrived. The author emphasizes the importance of compliance, ethics, and risk management practises in achieving success. He looks at how the board of directors may oversee company strategy, CEO remuneration, succession planning, crisis management, performance assessment, board composition, and even shareholder communications.

Through the prism of corporate compliance and strategy, this interesting book offers a fresh look at corporate bribery and corruption. It covers a wide range of topics, including regular corporate issues and bribery anecdotes, as well as examples of how unethical individuals invented unique bribery techniques. Corruption also draws attention to high-risk areas and industries, such as construction, healthcare, defence, and telecommunications. However, you should be aware that as you read this book, you may begin to suspect that no industry is truly devoid of bribery and corruption! Investors, lawmakers, and regulators are putting pressure on multinational firms to enhance their corporate governance, business sustainability, and corporate culture in today's economic climate. In today's global business climate, business sustainability, corporate governance, and organizational ethics are gaining centre stage. This long-awaited work delves deep into each of these three critical areas, helping readers achieve a thorough understanding through features such as chapter summaries, key words, discussion questions.

This book investigates the function of moral ideals as economic productive forces as well as the impact of ethical and immoral behaviour on the economy. It demonstrates how ethics boosts economic production and gives particular ethics tools for students and managers to use. Following that, it discusses ethical assessment methods to help the reader analyze economic behaviour ethically. The book finishes with a discussion of the relevance of ethics in the workplace and in the economy, as well as the ethics tools that management may use to encourage ethical behaviour among their staff.

It is vital to keep oneself up to date with in-depth knowledge in order to stay ahead of the competition. Any entrepreneur understands the value of acquiring such resources. It makes sense for a businessperson to have the most up-to-date business ethics book in their personal library, such as this one. This book stresses the real-world significance of crucial themes, including the essence of morality, main theories of ethics and economic justice, and contrasting perspectives on capitalism and corporate responsibility. It is comprehensive, adaptable, and designed to increase readers' engagement with the subject in order to improve their knowledge and understanding. Companies such as Facebook, Google, Wells Fargo, Volkswagen, and Amazon are featured in a variety of real-world case studies. Slow and rapid thinking, the inherent tension between the individual and the organization, conformity, and the problems of speaking the truth to power are all subjects treated in depth in this practical, down-to-earth text. As they wrestle with ethical challenges large and small, students and professionals are given abundant opportunities to participate in meaningful reflection, discussion, and application.

"The Ethical Roadmap" work is organized around interrelated layers of organizational behaviour, with an emphasis on ethics at the individual, group, and organizational levels. Students and professionals can practise their ethical reasoning skills through self-assessments, reflection features, and application projects.

In addition to business realities, the author offers a critical perspective on how these things can only be accomplished by harmonizing culture, strategy, compliance processes, and other perks like remuneration. The misconception that governance, risk management, and compliance are minor considerations in the inner workings of a company is refuted. In reality, it is the success of these efforts that contributes to total market gains, with the high-profile failures of huge banking institutions, large oil firms, and real estate used to demonstrate the point. Examples that depict real-life situations and allow readers to grapple with moral ambiguity. Students and professionals are challenged to see alternative moral views and practise ethical decision-making through discussion questions at the end of each chapter. This short, well-organized work will be a great tool for students and professionals taking corporate ethics courses to comprehend ethics in the digital era. Rather than flying over abstract notions and philosophical discussions at the treetop level, this book assists professionals by taking them on a tour through the tough world of business ethics at the ground level of the corporation. Employees can have a better understanding of how their corporate code of ethics connects to operational decisions made on a daily basis by evaluating topics and scenarios that directly relate to their work environment. Using his unique optimum ethical model, which defines how to select and educate ethical people, make ethical decisions, and establish a trustworthy, productive work environment, the author illustrates how to construct companies that encourage ethical conduct and eliminate ethical hazards. This work takes a practical approach, with suggestions, techniques, and real-world examples focusing on a wide range of enterprises, sectors, and concerns.

Acknowledgements

At the outset I will thank to my family for supporting me throughout the journey of writing my book and encouraging me to live my dreams- my son has always been instrumental in giving his inspiration to complete the writing of this book, Lastly, I would like to thank all the people whom I have been associated, you gave me power. At last thank you all for gifting your time to read out this book.

I'd want to convey my heartfelt appreciation to the Almighty God for bestowing his blessings and being so gracious.

CHAPTER ONE

INTRODUCTION

Bird's Eye View On The Ethical Roadmap

" Apart from the values and ethics that I have tried to live by, the legacy I would like to leave behind is a very simple one: that I have always stood up for what I consider to be the right thing, and I have tried to be as fair and equitable as I could be." -Ratan Tata

The business ethics movement has yet to persuade many individuals. There is a lot of evidence that unethical behaviour may harm a company's reputation and cause its stock price to drop. Furthermore, ethical businesses are more likely to create trust among your shareholders, workers, customers, and the general public, which is obviously beneficial to your bottom line. Given the ever-changing and difficult business VUCA (Volatility, Uncertainty, Complexity, and Ambiguity) landscape, making a profit is no longer the sole goal of running a company. Instead of reciprocating in a caring community, the environment has become a corporate need for long-term survival in this competitive world. Remember that in order to survive and develop in this competitive market, businesses must have solid corporate governance and adhere to all company regulations. Nowadays, the terms "ethical" and "sustainable" are frequently used in conjunction with discussions about branding and marketing. Consumers perceive brands as more trustworthy, reliable, and compassionate towards your larger community or society when you embrace superior principles, tactics, and activities. As a result, company owners should always assess the strength of their marketing methods as well as whether or not their image goes far enough to make a difference or look valuable to society. A firm that practises ethical marketing is more likely to instil a feeling of purpose in both its customers and employees.

In this book*"The ethical Roadmap"* of business and compliance investigates why rules-based, tick-box, defended compliance continues to fail, and proposes a new strategy for businesses that want to thrive and prosper. This book highlights the benefits that a really successful compliance and ethics programme can provide when it works hand in hand with a values-based culture of shared ownership, including competitive advantage, career happiness, employee and customer loyalty, and brand improvement. Corruption is nothing new, but as a culture, you're more aware of it and more willing to believe charges. Rather than brushing allegations under the floor or rejecting complaints, businesses are increasingly giving people who raise concerns a voice. However, you may be wondering what you can do to avoid corruption and unethical behaviour in the first place in your company.

This year, nearly every company in the world was compelled to rethink their marketing strategies in order to suit a market ravaged by the COVID-19-20 epidemic. Many businesses opted to do so by leading with their principles, acknowledging their consumers' issues, and guiding their approach with empathy. So, the bottom line is that firms that lead with a conscience are considerably more likely to be credited, trusted, and supported, which means that a values-driven approach is one of the most significant methods for brands to build a responsible marketing strategy.

Unlike past generations of consumers, today's generation is considerably more interested in learning about the companies they support. This involves understanding what their goods are composed of, who manufactures them, and the ethical framework that binds them together, as well as their general practises, environmental imprint, and other factors. If you want to *"do the right thing"* in business, you must first determine why you're doing what you're doing and what your desired objective is. Is it to win, appear good, or even wipe out the competition? Is it to redefine greatness, highlight outstanding abilities, or effect good change? Are you attempting to prove or exhibit who you are? The former will promote egotistical banter, but the latter will produce togetherness, pride, and exceptional performance. Business ethics is successful when human resources are used effectively and efficiently. Every day, corporations face difficult decisions about the right thing to do, but how can a business act ethically as an organization made up of individuals with diverse opinions and values? "*The Ethical Roadmap*" is a lively and entertaining introduction to the topic of corporate ethics. It provides practical counsel for handling ethical challenges in business, based on illustrative examples such as the Ford Pinto case, Enron, Walmart, and British Petroleum. presents readers with unsolved current case studies to ponder, encouraging them to participate in decision-making and make their own recommendations.

You're setting yourself and your staff up for failure if you think you can transform the culture of your department or business overnight. Instead, conceive large, strategic concepts and then put them into action in little, tactical, step-by-step, incremental steps. Sure, you're focusing on cultures that promote ethics, compliance, and accountability, but this strategy is essential for any culture change project. This book provides clear, detailed, and practical information for practitioners and decision-makers in any organization or corporation. It describes, in layman's words, the skills, tools, and attitude required to build and deliver a best-practice compliance and ethics program—one that complies with legal, stakeholder, and societal standards and protects your company from fines, penalties, and reputational harm. You'll need to understand how to employ ethical methods, make ethical judgments, and include the most up-to-date knowledge on ethics and governance scandals, legal liabilities, and professional accounting and auditing difficulties. To sustain stakeholder support and for auditors to examine financial statements, you must understand why building an ethical business culture is critical.

How you handle the ambiguities, the grey regions of ethics, which, as you've stated, aren't black and white, will decide your leadership effectiveness. How can you get the best outcome out of one bad scenario versus another bad situation? Because of the ethics scandals that have stopped companies and individuals from achieving their goals, businesses and the accounting profession have never been under such close ethical scrutiny. Understanding why ethical behaviour is so vital to achievement, as well as being aware of possible hazards, is critical to your own success. The notion that business is just about making money no longer holds water in the twenty-first century, as businesses all over the world are eschewing conventional distinctions in order to prosper. However, your expectations for businesses are still shaped by an out-of-date mentality that prioritises shareholder profits over everything else. This book tells a fresh story about the nature of business, illustrating how today's most influential ideas and businesses are united by a commitment to responsibility and ethics. This book is the first attempt to explain the circumstances that led to a focus on business ethics, particularly in the 2020 era, and how the broader field expanded to include related concepts like corporate governance, corporate social responsibility, ethical leadership, sustainable business, and responsible management education. *"The Ethical Roadmap"* provides an overview and analysis of key developments in contemporary business ethics by looking at them in terms of their diachronic development – key thinkers, key issues, and key institutions, as well as how they all contributed to current understandings of business ethics, governance, and practise.

It doesn't have to be a tough issue to discuss business ethics. Effective decision-making, policy development, and organizational management all hinge on a thorough grasp of the concepts that govern our daily lives. Explore the topic of corporate ethics via theory and examples from popular culture in this book. Learn how to properly negotiate the complex organizational morality of today's world with these practical recommendations. You all slip into moral quagmires without even realising it. *"The Ethical Roadmap"* educates business executives, students, and other readers on how to recognise these traps, avoid them, and dig their way out if they do fall into them. The author outlines some of the behaviours and expectations that may be implemented immediately in your firm to encourage ethical conduct from the top down. The author also shows ethics in action, such as how to cope with circumstances where the correct solution isn't obvious. The following business ethics objectives will be met by reading this book: ethical decision-making, deliberate blindness, individual ethics at work, unethical behaviour at work, and a method for dealing with unethical concerns. Author's examples give fantastic role-playing opportunities and possibilities to improve your grasp of soft skills like communication, persuasion, presentation, leadership, and a global attitude. Organizations continue to be harmed and taken down across the world as a result of systematic noncompliance or the sins of a few, and the media are full of stories of corporate scandals and crimes. This is despite growing ethical expectations from stakeholders, the ability of social media to expose businesses, the proliferation of compliance rules and regulations, and the growing number of policies, processes, and compliance officers put in place in response. So, why is it that compliance isn't working?

Each area of business, such as finance, governance, leadership, marketing, and human resource management, introduces the theory of virtue ethics and supports readers' understanding with chapter summaries, in-depth analysis, and real-life examples from a variety of nations. New case studies use real-world corporations like the NFL, Wells Fargo, Exxon Mobil, and Volkswagen to solve tough ethical challenges. Students and professional can wrestle with the grey regions of corporate ethics with new chapter-opening ethical problems based on real-life scenarios. In an increasingly complicated, multi-stakeholder environment, how can you be an ethical corporate citizen? This is the most critical question confronting today's enterprises, large and small, local and global. *"The Ethical Roadmap"* is a comprehensive yet approachable examination of the key ethical theories and how they relate to the primary stakeholders confronted with this issue. The biggest financial crisis in history, as well as the atrocious fraud, greed, and corruption that led to it, harmed not only the banking industry, but companies and individuals all across the world. It might have been avoided simply if optimal business procedures had been followed. For the past few years, the author's team and he have been exploring five key areas of focus: corporate ethics, government policy, ethical leadership, CSR, and whistleblowing. The author's purpose was to look at the best and worst management methods in these areas. People are where ethics may be found. In truth, the organization's ethics are represented by its leaders. The majority of businesses have a set of codified ethical guidelines. And although that gives advice, which is wonderful, whatever conduct emanates from the organization's executives symbolises the organization's ethics. As a result, the leaders are the organization's ethics. Whether you like it or not, you're representing a firm. Author set some priorities which include: prioritizing purpose above profit; producing value for stakeholders over shareholders; viewing business as anchored in society rather than markets; acknowledging people's complete humanity as well as their economic interests; and combining business and ethics into a more holistic approach. This book explains how ethical beliefs help people persevere in difficult circumstances and flourish in the long run, using examples from a variety of enterprises, sectors, and nations.

The prevalent idea that there are inescapable trade-offs between performing morally and flourishing financially is debunked by real-world success tales. A simple and straightforward guide to ethical business practises based on common-sense moral concepts. *"The Ethical Roadmap"* provides succinct solutions to the three most critical ethical problems faced by business professionals: What distinguishes good from bad business practises? Why do excellent, respectable entrepreneurs occasionally do the wrong thing? How can you utilise the answers to these questions to improve the behaviour of yourself, your coworkers, your supervisors, and your employees? In business, poor behaviour is rarely the product of bad intentions. Most individuals have good intentions most of the time.

A notorious example of this was the 2001 Enron affair, in which the American energy company was exposed for years of falsely reporting its financial accounts, with its accounting firm, Arthur Andersen, signing off on numbers that were erroneous. The misrepresentation had an impact on stockholder prices, and public stockholders lost more than $25 billion as a result of this ethical infringement. Both firms subsequently went out of business, and despite the fact that just a tiny part of the accounting firm's workers worked for Enron, the firm's demise resulted in the loss of 85,000 jobs. Corporate corruption tales abound in today's news. These accidents are frequently blamed on top-level decision-makers, and properly so in most situations. Modern business executives are responsible for both promoting ethical conduct and dealing with ethical snafus that arise during their term. You have a responsibility to fulfil. That assumption is that you would conduct yourself in an ethical manner and represent your company as such. As a result, this is a very crucial discussion that you should have. And the author wants to offer a set of principles and things to consider in your conversation so that you can go through that grey region with the best chance of success. And the author wants to offer a set of principles and things to think about in your debate so that you can go through that grey area with the best chance of coming up with a good, sound ethical solution. People are becoming increasingly aware of how you act as individuals and as corporations. If you act honestly, you'll have a solid reputation in the marketplace. If you don't behave ethically, you risk alienating the very individuals to whom you should be selling your goods. It would be so simple if ethics were a one-size-fits-all scenario. If you had to write and provide incorrect responses all of the time, One might be compared to the other. Go home, secure in the knowledge that you did the right thing. That is just not the case. In your respective nations, you have diverse cultures. Within a corporation, there are diverse cultures, and even within a country, there are different expectations.

Knowing the standards for where you are at the moment is crucial to understanding how you should act ethically or what defines ethical action. So there you have it: your company's culture. There's your country's culture. There are the laws in your own nation. From an ethical standpoint, there are the standards you've set, and being consistent in how you deal with your peers, customers, and management team to extend the idea of one size doesn't fit all from an ethical standpoint, and the reality that there isn't a right or wrong solution. Your access to knowledge on virtually any item, product, or service is limitless in the digital age.It's no longer possible for companies to hide behind false commercials, pitches, or trademarks.

Significant noncompliance failures are not usually the consequence of deliberate wrongdoing. Defects in corporate governance and risk management are sometimes to blame. Given the rapid rate of change and innovation in your sector, it's crucial to remember that you're here to leave an indelible mark. Your standards provide practical assistance for typical compliance issues, ensuring that your staff always have access to the most up-to-date ethical information. The layers of compliance processes are expanding at firms all around the world. At first glance, this appears to make sense: increasing the number of laws aimed at prohibiting unethical or harmful activity appears to be the most apparent and easy way of doing so. However, a checkbox mindset that creates the perception of risk reduction without actually doing so is one of the most disconcerting and unexpected outcomes of a sole concentration on ethics-as-compliance. Furthermore, unless taken carefully, a compliance-focused strategy to prevent unethical activity can stifle a company's ability to innovate and take calculated risks.

At its most basic level, cultural transformation is all about ensuring that you're only promoting behaviour that is completely consistent with your beliefs and goals. It's a seemingly easy notion, but, in practice, it may be exceedingly difficult to execute. Get some help if you don't know how to accomplish something or if you're not sure whether you're doing it correctly. Outside eyes and ears are typically better at recognizing where you could be promoting exactly the sort of behaviour you claim you want to stop, even if unwittingly.

Business ethics is a prominent subject in the media, society at large, and academics these days. Even corporations are adding ethical discussion into their internal discourse and governance procedures. How is it put into reality and how can it be reconciled with market competitiveness? Does it include people as aware beings with a sense of morality? For examples of scandals and questionable behaviour, look at Enron, Lehman Brothers, Volkswagen, Siemens, and France Télécom, as well as Bernie Madoff's Ponzi scheme. On the other hand, there are excellent instances of corporate ethics at work, such as François Michelin's people-centered vision, Bill George's leadership at Medtronic, and AES Corporation's basic values, which are still in use today.

Remember that in order to survive and develop in this competitive market, businesses must have solid corporate governance and adhere to all company regulations.

According to a shocking report released at the end of 2019, nearly one hundred Fortune 500 companies skipped paying federal taxes the previous year, including well-known names such as Amazon, Chevron, and Starbucks.According to data conducted by the anti-poverty organization Action Aid International, huge internet giants like Facebook, Google, and Microsoft have all failed to pay taxes in poor nations where governments struggle to satisfy basic healthcare and educational needs.

Digital marketers now have a plethora of tools at their disposal to acquire massive amounts of data from their customers and develop richer, more personalised marketing methods. Consumers have rightfully grown more anxious about what happens to their personal data when they offer it to the firms with whom they do business in an age where notions such as surveillance capitalism and targeted advertising dominate practically every part of the Internet.

More individuals than ever before are concerned about their societal effect in today's environment. In the age of COVID-19, it's safe to say that ethical marketing has taken on a whole new meaning. In the course of a year, brands have been compelled to make fast adjustments to their marketing tactics and how they pivot their services towards their customers. While it may appear that the crisis has brought effective marketing initiatives to a halt, other research suggests otherwise.

It's easy to ignore a new technology's potential drawbacks when it arrives with significant advantages. Technology has come to control much of our modern work and personal lives. While technological advancements have allowed us to work from home, acquire a wide range of goods, occupy ourselves, and even receive remote medical treatment, they have also raised severe concerns. Concerns about anything from privacy to human behaviour to the environment are paired with the evident advantages of broad technology use. While executives are among the most enthusiastic supporters of technology solutions to problems, they are also acutely aware of the ethical issues that come with them.

Summing Up

There is a lot of evidence that unethical behaviour may harm a company's reputation and cause its stock price to drop. Ethical businesses are more likely to create trust among their shareholders, workers, customers, and the general public, which is obviously beneficial to their bottom line. Remember that in order to survive and develop in this competitive market, businesses must have solid corporate governance and adhere to all company regulations. In the age of COVID-19-20, it's safe to say that ethical marketing has taken on a whole new meaning. From an ethical standpoint, and the reality that there isn't a right or wrong solution, one size doesn't fit all. Ethical brands have been forced to make fast adjustments to their marketing tactics and how they pivot their services towards their customers.

CHAPTER TWO

ETHICAL LEADERSHIP

Leading With Positive Ethical Values And Bringing Out The Best In People

"At its best, leadership development is not an "event." It's a capacity-building endeavor. It's a process of human growth and development."

— Linda Fisher Thornton

What is the definition of ethical leadership? It's all about instilling the appropriate habits. It's all about doing the right thing when faced with a problem. We can see the behaviour that happens, but we can't see the values that lead to that behaviour. Values are the unseen forces that influence our actions. They have an impact on our views, and our attitudes have an impact on our ethical behaviour. An ethical behavioural chain is formed by the relationship between values, attitudes, and behaviour. It is critical to recognize that the first stage of ethical leadership is to establish the ethical tone from the top in order to shape the desired employee behaviours in the firm.

It's more critical than ever to ensure that, as a leader, your ethical message is consistent in today's high-visibility environment with the continual social media onslaught. Anyone may walk the talk, but if you don't sincerely believe in the value of ethical behaviour in your professional life, it will show to your colleagues, peers, and the individuals in the C-suite. Ethical leadership entails corporate executives acting ethically both within and outside of the workplace. According to the Harvard Business Review, ethical leaders will not overlook misconduct even if it is beneficial to their companies. Integrity and doing the right thing are keys to becoming an ethical leader. Ethical leaders serve as role models for the rest of the organization. To be an ethical leader, you must act ethically all of the time and throughout time, not only while others are watching. Doing the right thing all of the time, especially when it's tough, should be ingrained in a leader's DNA. It's unavoidable that you'll be found out if you act ethically in public yet evade responsibilities, cut costs, and prioritise business above people behind closed doors.

In modern times, corporate indiscretion, malfeasance, and deviance are constantly in the news and all around us. There isn't a day that goes by without news of a new organizational flaw. Organizations in every sector of society, both in India and throughout the world, consistently disappoint and frustrate us in terms of ethical grandeur. Much of what we view as the shadow or dark side of organizational behaviour is frequently difficult to grasp and appreciate. It baffles me how extremely committed, conscientious, and skilled middle-level executives or astute, successful, and powerful CEOs can cross the line and do such stupid things that jeopardise their jobs, wealth, reputation, families, and careers.

The behaviour or response of a leader in any particular event has an impact on future organizational behaviour in comparable situations, either strengthening or weakening its overall ethical substance. For example, if a high-performing employee cheats on the cost account and the boss overlooks it because of the person's good performance, the employee's desire to cheat will be increased. Employees, in particular, want to be led by people who have a moral operating system that is based on stated principles. Over time, this approach has become a model of ethics for the whole corporation. It is vital that the reaction of the individual leader be consistent with his or her championed ideals, morally grounded procedures, and declared behavioural standards.Actions speak louder than words in ethics, and they generate a buzz at the intermediate and junior levels. Value-centered reactions that are consistent help to foster ethical organizational behaviour. Established behavioural standards also aid in highlighting those areas that a leader wishes to emphasise as crucial in building a pattern of ethical behaviour based on the existing ethical state of the organization.

In terms of the second driver, ethical behaviour, a thorough ethics program is required to improve organizational members' ethical behaviour. The essential parts of an ethics program include: evaluation of the organization's underlying beliefs and philosophies; conformity with the organization's structures, procedures, and policies; and fulfilment of senior leadership's ethical goals. Based on these essentials, an ethics curriculum with the following elements can be built: Is this correct?A formal ethical code; the formation of an ethics committee; the appointment of an ethics officer; an ethics communication system; an ethics training program; and a system for tracking and managing consequences.The term "code of ethics" refers to a written declaration of an organization's permitted range of behaviours and acts. It consists of a written set of guidelines that must be followed by executives and other staff. A board-level ethics committee should be created to oversee how ethically a company conducts its operations and to indicate that ethical issues are taken seriously. The duty of overseeing the ethics program might then be entrusted to a specialised employee chosen specifically for the task. Hence, ethics is all about communication and education. Hence, other elements like ethics, communication, and training systems are important. Furthermore, a proper system for transgressors' repercussions management should be put in place.

Principles of Ethical Leadership

Leaders are aware of their influence on others and are concerned about it. They pay attention to others, are accepting of differing viewpoints, and treat people as ends in themselves, never as a means to a purpose. Leaders have a responsibility to serve and lead in a servant-like manner. They put the interests of others ahead of their own and act in ways that benefit others. They are concerned about others‘ well-being and engage in activities such as mentorship, empowerment, and team building. A leader who establishes a common vision for an effort by first doing a *"listening tour"* to determine what his people require and value for.

- When making decisions, leaders prioritize fairness and justice, which includes exhibiting fairness to individuals as well as the greater society. When it comes to hiring employees, setting salaries, or selecting external service providers, they must insist on fair and transparent methods.
- They display honesty and integrity, which aids in the development of trust, the strengthening of relationships, and the development of personal authority.
- They are also open and honest in their contacts with others, as well as diplomatic and understanding of others' needs.
- They also stick to their obligations. A leader who admits to making a mistake and accepts responsibility for it is.

A leader who recognizess an opportunity to solve a greater, broader societal problem by addressing a local problem that directly affects them and joins with other leaders to establish an effort that helps the broader community. In recent years, you've heard a lot about compassionate leadership, but 2020 has been a true test of how firms can combine it with ethical leadership. Being an ethical leader entails more than merely declaring your intention to behave in the best interests of everybody. Make an active strategy for how your job behaviour may help you become a more ethical leader. If you make a commitment, you will go to great lengths to maintain it. Through training opportunities, ethical behaviour should constantly be stressed. Schedule workshops that emphasize the importance of treating people ethically in the workplace. Be open and honest in all business transactions. If your organization has to shrink, for example, notify employees well in advance. More than ideals are required for ethical leadership. Care, justice, honesty, and respect are the raw materials of ethical leadership, but you must be transformed into effective acts in complicated and dynamic settings through a manufacturing process. As a result, you can deduce that ethical leaders adhere to what may be universal values such as fairness, equality, and respect, and extend these leadership principles beyond the business context. Furthermore, ethical leaders strive for it!! Elon Musk is one of the world's wealthiest people, with a net worth of more than $221 billion as of March, 2022, and is regarded as an innovator, with initiatives like Tesla, SpaceX, and the Hyperloop, among others. Musk has donated millions of dollars to charitable organizations and has his own foundation, the Musk Foundation, which has helped with hurricane and tsunami relief, as well as the Future of Life Institute, which aims to ensure that future artificial intelligence applications are beneficial to humanity. Ethical leadership necessitates the presence of ethical leaders. Leaders that are ethical may guarantee that ethical practises are followed across the company. Because leaders are inherently in a position of authority both on and off the job, ethical leadership must concentrate on how they use that power in their decisions, actions, and ways of influencing others. Leaders are in charge of persuading followers to do specific acts, accomplish tasks, and act in certain ways. As they support the internalisation of the corporate vision, effective leaders also influence processes, inspire change in attitudes and values, and enhance the empowerment and self-efficacy of their followers. The nurturing part of leadership may also help to boost an organization's culture and employee values to more ethical levels. As a result, ethical leadership linked to ideas like trust, honesty, thoughtfulness, charm, and justice. Except for the introduction of charm, much of this is logic. Ethical leaders don't need charisma; in fact, data reveals that many charismatic leaders have persuaded their followers to abandon their principles and convictions. Even more concerning is the reality that history is littered with charismatic leaders who rank poorly on the scale of ethical leadership. You foster a high degree of integrity by exhibiting ethical leadership, which promotes a sense of trustworthiness and inspires subordinates to embrace and follow our vision. Other personal attributes that guide your ethical ideas, attitudes, and judgments are founded on character and integrity. Ethical leaders are likely to be people-oriented and conscious of the consequences of their decisions. As a result, you use your influence and authority to serve the greater good rather than self-serving goals, resulting in a "win/win" situation for both employees and the company. This role modelling acts as a guide and motivation for others to prioritize the group's needs and interests over your own.

The Characteristics of Ethical Leaders

- Fairness is practised by ethical leaders by ensuring that everyone is treated fairly and equitably.
- Ethical leaders adhere to a set of consistent, widely held values or principles, such as honesty, fairness, respect, caring for others, accountability for one's actions, prioritizing the greater good over one's personal interests, and so on.
- Ethical leaders encourage ethical behaviour in the workplace and prohibit unethical behavior. Ethical leaders incorporate ethical considerations into their decision-making processes.
- Ethical leaders accept responsibility for both their successes and failures.

- They respect others, which is one of the characteristics of an ethical leader. An ethical leader should not use his or her followers to attain personal objectives.
- They are servant to others. An ethical leader should prioritize the needs of his followers before his own. They should be compassionate.
- They are just and fair. Wherever certain followers are treated differently, the basis for such treatment should be fair, transparent, and moral.

- They foster community. An ethical leader thinks about his own objectives as well as the aspirations of his followers and strives to attain goals that are beneficial to both. He puts forth more effort to achieve the community's objectives.
- They are dependable and trustworthy. Honest leaders may be trusted and counted on at all times. They consistently gain the respect of their fans.
- Individual respect implies that the leader respects everyone's moral standards. Nobody's values are superior or inferior to anybody else's. The leader may build confidence in an organization by valuing the individual. The golden rule comes to mind as the best example: treat others the way you want to be treated. If a leader respects himself or herself, he or she will respect others.
- Effective communication is essential for ethical leadership.
- Ethical standards should be clearly stated and individuals should be aware of them.
- Even when painful judgments must be made, the decision-making process should be publicly shared.
- Ethics should be addressed not only in times of crisis or major decision-making, but also in day-to-day operations.
- The leader must be able to build strong bonds with his or her followers. These connections must be built on the foundations of trust, respect, and open communication.
- Ethical leadership should be more inclusive of ethics.
- Organizations should think about doing the right thing not simply in terms of following the rules, but also in terms of social justice and sustainability.
- Everyone on the team should be aware of the framework and the significance of ethical behavior, and they should act accordingly.
- Rather than focusing on what ethical leadership should not be, the emphasis should be on developing and enforcing the appropriate model and framework for ethical leadership.
- Ethical leaders take their jobs seriously and wish to be successful in them.

- They also wish to assist in the empowerment of others and guarantee the success of the company and subordinates they serve.
- The ethical leader emphasizes the importance of hard work and devotion in completing the task.
- An ethical leader aspires to be defined and thought of as a decent person. There is a worry about doing the right thing and, maybe more crucially, thinking about what the appropriate action is.
- Ethical leaders are welcoming to everybody. This indicates that they are receptive to other viewpoints and encourage employees to share their thoughts. But, in addition to this kind of communicative and collaborative inclusion, ethical leaders interact with individuals from all walks of life.
- An ethical leader recognizess the value of a diverse workplace and strives to make the organization more inclusive of people of many nationalities, colours, cultures, and backgrounds.
- An ethical leader will talk about the high ideals and standards they have for themselves, their team, and the organization on a frequent basis.

Knowing your underlying principles and having the guts to follow them in all aspects of your life in the service of the greater good is what ethical leadership entails. In author's view, ethical leadership means leading in a way that respects others' rights and dignity, a concept that might be at odds with more traditional leadership paradigms. The major purpose of leadership in the past was to boost production and profitability. However, in the twenty-first century, this viewpoint has begun to fade as more organizational development and human resources professionals say that leaders are equally responsible for upholding moral and ethical norms. Therefore, good leadership entails not just ability but also ethics that alter companies and people's lives.

Challenges in Ethical Leadership

For today's leaders, ethical leadership is critical. The significance of being ethical in business and in life has been highlighted by the news in recent months and years. So, what can you do to make sure you're a principled leader who's building an ethical company? Begin by having an open conversation with your leadership team, assisting them in discovering and claiming their fundamental values, and then working together to construct a vision for how your world may be different using the 3-V Model. The author proposes a 3-V Model of Ethical Leadership as a framework for aligning leaders' internal beliefs and values with their exterior behaviours and actions for the greater good of workers, leaders, companies, and society.

- Vision: Ethical leadership necessitates the capacity to frame our activities inside an image of *"what should be"*—especially when it comes to serving others.
- Voice: Ethical leaders must be able to convey their vision to others in a genuine way that motivates people to take action. Ethical leaders try to do the correct and good things.
- Virtue: Ethical leaders demonstrate virtue by asking themselves, *"How do my values, vision, and voice match with and promote the common good?"* Owners, the C Suite, and senior management should create an atmosphere in which people have the discipline and strength to regularly select virtue; virtue will then become a habit that will get stronger with practise.

What was once widely acknowledged as good and true, just and just, is now a point of contention. It is extremely difficult for values-based leaders to thrive in an atmosphere of relativism. Starting from the top down is the only way to develop an ethical business. Your workers will pick up on your actions, decisions, and ideals and apply them to their own work. Leading by example instils respect and shows your staff that you believe in them and are confident in their abilities. As the expression goes, you can't pour from an empty cup. Leaders who look after themselves are more likely to manage and care for others effectively. As a leader, you will undoubtedly face difficulties. The way you cope with and overcome these obstacles shapes who you are as people and the image you project to others. your *"moral values"* determine how you as individuals display a code of behaviour that is acceptable and suitable.

Ethical leadership means examining your moral values and how you apply them in your daily lives. This shows your leadership beliefs and successes. You can accept responsibility for your decisions and comprehend the necessity of openness if you are able to accept accountability for your decisions. Consider this scenario: you've been asked to make a game-changing decision that makes you feel uneasy. Your job is on the line, and if you don't make a choice, you may lose it. You know from a slew of studies that ethically-driven decision-making and leadership foster credibility, respect, process, motives, and trust, as well as a positive environment in which employees, customers, and suppliers engage in profitable long-term relationships that benefit all stakeholders. Of course, psychopathic narcissists can benefit in the short run; just look at Bernard Madoff's case. His Ponzi scheme fell apart after years of *"ripping people off"* and living an incredibly luxurious life, and he was sentenced to a number of lifetimes in jail for his immoral conduct. Although the German carmaker has a history of cultivating a competitive corporate culture, Martin Winterkorn, the company's CEO since 2007, may have contributed to a culture that allowed the installation of software that failed to correctly detect emissions on its vehicles. Winterkorn appears to have been renowned as a hard-driving perfectionist who would go about with a gauge in his hand to measure gaps between vehicle doors in his tireless quest for the top rank among global auto makers, despite his claims that he was unaware of the misconduct. Bad actions, motivated by the need for immediate gratification, frequently result in unfavourable long-term consequences. Being a long-term business leader who is ethical is also the most effective strategy to defend and grow a company. You've been monitoring headlines about British Home Stores, Toyota, Rolls-Royce, BT, Samsung, Toshiba, Toyota, and a variety of other corporations in recent months, and you've been wondering where all the ethically-driven corporate executives have gone. Your personal-promotion of conduct to your people through effective two-way communication, encouragement of excellent behaviour, and reflecting your beliefs through your decision-making are all examples of ethical leadership. By accepting responsibility for your decisions and realizing the significance of transparency, you motivate people to follow your lead. To become this style of leader, you must analyze your values, thoughts, and objectives honestly. Ethical leaders who take responsibility for this have a greater understanding of how their own activities influence and impact others. Understanding the significance of a cultural framework that others gladly follow creates a successful platform. Individuals may better grasp the influence of corrective behaviour, both individually and at work, by educating people about prevalent ethical challenges occurring throughout the world, governance frameworks, and other significant elements. Now, there are a number of business endeavours and things going on that aren't ready for public consumption, if you will, and you must respect that because stories circulate and things may get out of hand. As a result, you won't always be able to share everything. Discarding something because of the character of the person who could deliver it to you is a very, very dangerous trap. So, it's easy to get caught up in your day-to-day work as a leader and forget about these traps. People are where ethics may be found. In truth, the organization's ethics are represented by its leaders. The majority of businesses have a set of codified ethical guidelines. And although that gives advice, and it's a wonderful thing that it does, whatever conduct emanates from the organization's executives symbolizes the organization's ethics. Every leader, at some time, will fall into an ethical trap. The first is attempting to soften the shock of terrible news or prospective bad news by lying or coming dangerously close to lying as a result. Let me give you an illustration. Let's imagine your organization is going through a cost-cutting or resource-allocation process, or whatever phrase you choose to use.

Given the macro-changes influencing your society, the demand for ethical leadership will grow in the next few years. Leaders in most industries will encounter complexity, fast change, fierce competition, globalization, disruption, and new technologies in the near future. Leaders will need to handle ethical difficulties around hard subjects like artificial intelligence, managing people's private data, robots, and genetic engineering, to mention a few, in this context. As a result, you still have a long way to go in terms of closing the gap between existing practise and the capacity you'll need in the near future in terms of ethical leadership. Leaders and followers form an intellectual and emotional bond as a result of such involvement, making both sides equally accountable in the pursuit of mutual goals. Cohorts are also coached by ethical leaders in developing a sense of personal and professional competence, which helps them thrive while also being more resilient, loyal, and lucrative. Employees look up to morally-minded role models where and when they see them at work. There is a strong link between a personally motivated moral conscience, business ethics, and long-term company success.

Your Checklist: An Ethical Leader

Leaders who are successful add value. As an ethical leader, embracing ownership and accountability for adding value is critical to your personal and organizational success. Having a strong commitment to establishing a communication flow and leading by example will foster loyalty and productivity. You're confident that the majority of you can think of a few immoral decisions.

- You exhibit a strong dedication to ethical and moral ideals
- You communicate ethical standards to members in a clear and concise manner
- You Set an example of ethical behaviour in your decisions and behavior
- You are trustworthy and can be relied upon to tell the truth
- You acts on your stated values "*walk the talk*"
- You distribute work to members in a fair and impartial manner

- You can be counted on to keep promises and obligations
- You are adamant about doing what is right and fair, even when it is difficult
- You recognize and accept responsibility for mistakes made
- You believe that honesty and integrity are important personal qualities for ethical leaders
- You lead by example in terms of devotion and self-sacrifice for the company
- You disapprove of the use of unethical methods to improve performance
- When evaluating member performance and awarding awards, it is fair and objective
- You put the needs of others ahead of your own
- Your team members are held accountable for adhering to ethical standards in their work

"Effective leaders focus on what's right and exemplify to their people that they are there to help, and not to exploit the vulnerabilities of others," she said. "Their organizations typically respond to their example and their desire to serve others and make a positive difference" – Thornton

It is the responsibility of an ethical leader to communicate with each team member while also allowing for free discussion, since some people may have questions or concerns that need to be addressed. Ethical leaders who set a good example may inspire others to follow suit. People are generally influenced by the interactions that take place around them. Positive coworker communication may have an impact on workplace productivity and attitude. Ethical leaders may contribute to the creation of a pleasant atmosphere with constructive interactions on three levels: the person, the team, and the company as a whole. Ethical leadership can also include managing a team's behaviour and collaboration. A strong ethical leader's role includes maintaining a pleasant work environment. Ethical leaders collaborate and develop succession plans for their organizations to ensure the organization's long-term prosperity. Instead of continually re-thinking and assessing the issue, an ethical framework assists a leader and the company in making decisions and approaching activities with a cohesive strategy. Although a framework will not always provide ethical leaders with a clear answer, it will make it simpler to assess the circumstances and listen to other people's perspectives on the subject.

What values are motivating decision-making in companies as they navigate uncertain times ahead? With what has unfolded before us in 2020, the importance of ethical leadership has never been greater. This year has been particularly difficult for airlines and hotels, and you can look to the sector for another wonderful example of ethical leadership from the former CEO of Japan Airlines. Haruka Nishimatsu was a CEO who rode the bus to work and ate lunch with his coworkers in the office canteen. He didn't hide in the ivory towers; instead, he made himself available to his whole team. When things were rough a decade ago, he accepted a substantial wage cut to earn less than his pilots. If his employees had to suffer, he made sure he did as well. Kazuo Inamori, Nishimatsu's replacement, went one step further by refusing to take a salary while successfully turning JAL into a profitable airline. A leader motivates and encourages his or her subordinates and followers to work together to achieve a shared objective, whether it's teamwork, corporate goals, or a project. Because everyone of his subordinates has a distinct personality, it is the leader's ethical responsibility to treat them with respect. Because leaders hold a significant position in the organization and have an impact on the development of organizational values, they shape and develop the ethical environment.

Current Scenario

In today's economic world, moral and ethical leadership are critical. It is critical to have a system in place to ensure ethical behaviour at all levels. Ethical and moral leadership are also included in the social responsibility area. This is about doing what is right and moral in the eyes of the public, as well as having a plan in place to ensure ethical decision-making. It is critical to have a leader who is truthful, not only to himself but also to others. When a leader is truthful, the organization gains a sense of transparency and, as a result, trust. Cost-cutting tactics within a company are an example. The best way to be honest with employees and establish confidence is to provide facts up front to the organization about why these layoffs are occurring and strategies to reorganise roles to either maintain jobs or fill unfilled positions. Stakeholders include everyone in the organization. Everyone has a stake in the company, from employees to consumers. It is critical to have an open dialogue with employees in order to support ethical behaviour. According to leaders, profits must not come before stakeholders. This does not imply that the firm is deliberately losing money. Obviously, the corporation exists to generate a profit. This implies that choices must be made with the best interests of all parties in mind. A sales company, for example, could increase its sales force's annual targets. The objectives are unachievable, and no one receives a bonus. This may result in employee dissatisfaction and mistrust. Adjusting goals and increasing bonus payouts are the correct steps to take to enhance employee motivation. A leader is responsible for creating an organization that resembles a close-knit community. Everyone in a company is working toward a common objective if the leader creates a feeling of community. Take, for example, a pharmaceutical firm. The company's overall objective is to generate a profit. The leader's first priority, however, must be to communicate that the patient comes first and that the treatment will benefit the patient. Profits will follow if the drug benefits the patient. The group will develop a feeling of community if the leader establishes a shared aim. It is critical for leaders to operate morally and ethically in today's corporate world. This provides workers with internal transparency and fosters a sense of trust in the organization's executives. The organization can function as a cohesive entity that acts ethically by having its leaders act ethically and having a plan to ensure ethical leadership. The moral and ethical leader does not market himself or herself as ethical. The moral and ethical leader sets an example for others to follow. They also carry out socially responsible details. They do things behind the scenes that go unseen yet are crucial to their success as ethical leaders.

Traditional corporate leadership styles have simply paid lip service to controlling the social context in which businesses function up until now. Today's company leaders may be losing out on a wonderful chance to *"future-proof"* their organizations by utilising new digitised technology to build workplaces where people flourish because their social requirements are addressed. Many people see that today's traditional business structures are out of step with major technological advancements that have dissolved corporate borders and connected suppliers and customers into a sharing economy, whether it's Uber, Airbnb, or crowdfunding. Many businesses‘ success is being sabotaged by old methods of thinking and doing. The new ethical leadership paradigm that requires employees to release discretionary effort differs significantly from previous models. It prioritizes employees and produces results as a result of their degrees of involvement. Despite this, annual employee engagement surveys show that CEOs are hesitant to actively and purposefully construct their company's culture. Too many organizations' ideals are unoperationalized, and their cultures are dysfunctional due to a lack of managerial consistency. Thankfully, ethical leadership is not the same as ordinary leadership. You may anticipate new workers continuing to vote with their feet and quit their companies after 1 or 2 years in pursuit of more rewarding work if leaders fail to adopt the new ethical leadership paradigm. Organizations now operate in a highly competitive and dynamic environment, which forces them to alter their organizational structures on a regular basis. However, the success of change programs may be hampered by employee resistance, particularly if they are unprepared to change. While ethical leaders who serve as guides and give support can help boost workers‘ readiness to change, ethical leaders who serve as guides and offer support can also make a difference by lowering ambiguity.

However, there is virtually little study on the function of ethical leadership in improving employees' willingness to change.

Advantages Of Practising Ethical Leadership

Ethical leadership is a management approach that may be applied to any company. The following are the most significant advantages for a firm that values ethical leadership:

- When employees work for an ethical boss, their morale rises
- Staff will not feel as though they are assisting a crooked individual in accumulating even more wealth
- Ethical leaders have the ability to motivate others who work with them to achieve their full potential
- Ethical executives do not harm a company's reputation
- Company scandals can harm a company's reputation and drive consumers to switch to a rival
- Companies that appoint ethical executives are more likely to retain both staff and consumers

As a result, it is linked to ideas like trust, honesty, thoughtfulness, charm, and justice. Ethical leadership is a type of leadership in which people act in a way that is acceptable and suitable for the greater good in all aspects of their lives. Ethical leadership is a leadership paradigm that applies the aforementioned ethical ideals to the management of subordinates. Because ethics is concerned with the principles of *"good"* behaviour and leadership is concerned with persuading others to attain a goal, ethical leadership is influencing others via ethics. People are more prone to assessing others based on their actions than their words. Ethical leaders may acquire the respect of their peers by exercising and displaying ethical, honest, and selfless behaviour towards their subordinates. People are more inclined to follow a leader who is trustworthy and respects others.

If you expect your employees to treat everyone with respect, you can't expect them to take you seriously if you make fun of them or gossip about them. If you're prepared to break the rules for the sake of convenience, the same applies. If your company is compelled to follow federal and state rules, for example, your employees will be upset if labour standards or environmental restrictions are broken. Employees will pick up on your hypocrisy and regard your company's goal and vision as a public façade. Ethics is a difficult subject. You must develop clear policies in the form of mission statements, rules, laws, and practices to ensure clarity. Employees require written copies of the following policies from the moment they are employed. These must also be documented in an easy-to-understand manner that is devoid of exploitable flaws. If you're stuck for ideas, consider basing your company's vision and policies on the visions and policies of other firms that you admire or find successful. You may also engage a consultant to examine your company and recommend the best course of action. The culture and atmosphere of the workplace can also pose a threat to ethical leadership. When faced with moral grey zones, ethical leadership may be extremely tough. In situations like these, doing the right thing may be counterproductive to your company's financial line. You're ready to grow, but new safety standards mandate that you replace the organization's equipment, which will cost you money. You can reason that your present equipment is acceptable and that breaking the laws in this one instance would enhance profits and allow you to hire additional people in the community. To put it another way, the ends justify the methods. However, if an injured worker sues you after learning that you deliberately disobeyed safety standards, you might face major legal trouble. An ethical leader recognizes that an organization's worldwide market competitiveness is determined by three factors: quality product, quality customer service, and quality delivery.

Role Of An Ethical Leader

The role of ethical leadership must be taken seriously and with respect. As previously said, you may demonstrate real ethical leadership and so develop confidence among your subordinates by doing what you say. As a leader, you must take responsibility for your actions and decisions. An ethical leader must think about all of his or her activities and figure out how to do the least amount of harm possible. Ethical leaders will frequently be confronted with circumstances in which both actions have the potential to bring good or harm, but they must be mindful of picking the *"best"* response for the scenario while keeping in mind their general ethical framework and the organization's purpose. In order to be ethical, a leader must be consistent in his or her approach. By adhering to his or her own ethical standards, an ethical leader can encourage his or her employees. You must also be consistent in your treatment of subordinates and stakeholders.When dealing with others, you must lay forth the norms and ethical framework and adhere to them. You can't scold someone for doing something you wouldn't do in a different scenario. Leaders who are ethical must learn to be authoritative and to leverage their influence. However, there are significant differences between how autocratic or authoritarian leaders use authority and how ethical leaders manage their employees. Whereas more authoritarian leadership approaches place decision-making in the hands of the leader, ethical leadership requires teamwork.It does not imply that the ethical leader would not make the ultimate choice; rather, it suggests that power is organised in such a manner that others can share it with the leader. It should go without saying that someone who is ethical is also trustworthy and loyal. Within the organization, ethical leaders build a feeling of community and team spirit. When an ethical leader sets out to achieve goals, it's not simply about achieving personal objectives. Because followers trust honest and trustworthy leaders, being honest is especially vital for becoming an effective ethical leader. A moral leader is always kind and fair. They don't play favourites and treat everyone the same. No employee should be afraid of being treated unfairly because of their gender, race, nationality, or any other factor under the leadership of an ethical leader. Respect for followers is one of the most crucial characteristics of ethical leadership. Employees grow and develop under the leadership of an ethical leader. Employees are rewarded for coming up with novel ideas and encouraged to go above and above to enhance how things are done. Employees are commended for taking the initiative rather than waiting for someone else to do it. All choices made by ethical leaders are double-checked to verify that they are in line with the organization's overarching principles. Only those choices that match this requirement are implemented. Ethical leadership is more than simply talking the talk; it also entails doing the walk. The high expectations that an ethical leader has for his or her staff also apply to individuals. By leading by example, leaders expect others to follow suit. They guarantee that there is uniform knowledge across the organization by communicating and debating values on a regular basis. Employees who work under an ethical leader are expected to do the right thing all of the time, not just when it is convenient for them.

Individuals communicate in a variety of ways. Others may be afraid to talk with a leader because of fear, anxiety, or just not understanding how to explain what they are attempting to say in public, regardless of who they are dealing with or the scenario. As an ethical leader, it's critical to teach others about ethics, especially when they're confronted with an ethical dilemma at work. One responsibility of an ethical leader is to focus on the general relevance of ethics, including ethical standards and other ethical challenges, and how these elements might impact society. It is critical for leaders to foster camaraderie among their employees. Trust, fairness, honesty, openness, compassion, and respect are all qualities that characterize good partnerships. It's easy to lose sight of what your firm stands for as your company expands. As your firm grows, it might be tough to guarantee that all of your employees obey the rules and embody your company's goal, vision, and values. Understanding how to overcome some of the obstacles to ethical leadership can not only helps you preserve goodwill with the public and stakeholders, but it may also help you avoid future difficulties. One of the most difficult aspects of ethical leadership is the ability to stick to the rules you set for your company. Following your own ethical code serves as an example to your staff, demonstrating that you are committed to them. Following your own ethical code inspires your colleagues by demonstrating that you are committed to your fundamental beliefs. Ethics-based leadership techniques such as genuine and ethical leadership had similar associations with a wide range of positive employee outcomes as transformational leadership (e.g., trust in supervisor, engagement, and job satisfaction).Furthermore, their meta-analytic study discovered that the more emphasis leaders place on ethics, the better their ability to predict positive outcomes. They also found that ethical leadership is significantly positively related to employee task performance, even in the presence of transformational leadership. As a result, ethical leadership may have a role to play in anticipating a valued outcome in the workplace, such as willingness to change, which has been practically untapped until now.

Summing Up

Ethical leadership entails corporate executives acting ethically both within and outside of the workplace. Being an ethical leader entails more than merely declaring your intention to behave in the best interests of everybody. Ethical leaders are likely to be people-oriented and conscious of the consequences of their decisions. Ethical leaders encourage ethical behaviour in the workplace and prohibit unethical behavior. Leading by example instils respect and shows your staff that you believe in them and are confident in their abilities. Every leader, at some time, will fall into an ethical trap. Ethical leaders have a greater understanding of how their own activities influence and impact others. One of the most difficult aspects of ethical leadership is the ability to stick to the rules you set for your company. Following your own ethical code inspires your colleagues by demonstrating that you are committed to your fundamental beliefs. Ethical leadership may have a role to play in anticipating a valued outcome in the workplace, such as willingness to change.

CHAPTER THREE

CORPORATE GOVERNANCE

Organizational Structured Rules, Practices, and Processes

"I am not bound to win, but I am bound to be true. I am not bound to succeed, but I am bound to live by the light that I have. I must stand with anybody that stands right, and stand with him while he is right, and part with him when he goes wrong." – Abraham Lincoln

Corporate governance is a system of rules, regulations, and processes that regulate the direction and control of a firm. Corporate governance encompasses the relationships between the many stakeholders as well as the goals for which the organization is managed.*"Corporate Governance"* is the use of best management practises, strict respect of the word and spirit of the law, and adherence to ethical standards for successful wealth management and distribution. When there is a separation of ownership and control, corporate governance refers to the collection of systems that impact the decisions made by management. The Board of Directors, institutional shareholders, and the functioning of the market for corporate control are examples of these monitoring systems. Corporate governance refers to how a corporation is run to guarantee that all of its stakeholders receive a fair share of the company's profits and assets. Good corporate governance entails a company's commitment to operating its operations in a lawful, ethical, and transparent manner—a commitment that must start at the top and spread across the organization. Corporate governance is a system of rules, policies, and processes that guide the Board of Directors and independent committees in their monitoring and management of a firm. It entails balancing the needs of a company's stakeholders, which include management, workers, suppliers, customers, and the community, with the requirement to produce value for its shareholders and owners. Having a solid, active governance programme is essential for an organization's long-term financial health, development, and success.

Definition of corporate governance by the *Institute of Company Secretaries of India* is *"Corporate Governance is the application of best Management practices, Compliance of law in true letter and spirit and adherence to ethical standards for Effective Management and distribution of wealth and discharge of social Responsibility for sustainable development of all stakeholders"*.

Corporate governance makes businesses more responsible and transparent to investors, and it equips them with the tools they need to address genuine stakeholder concerns, including long-term environmental and social development. Increased access to finance promotes new investments, boosts economic growth, and creates job possibilities, all of which contribute to development. Corporate governance is to create an organization that optimises shareholder wealth. It envisions a company that prioritises satisfying social commitments to stakeholders over maximising profits. Shareholders, debt holders, trade creditors, suppliers, consumers, and communities affected by the corporation's activity are the primary external stakeholder groups in today's corporations. Any of the policies and practises that manage a firm can be referred to as corporate governance, but that definition falls short of describing what corporate governance actually is. It's more accurate to state that *"governance"* refers to the policies and procedures that enable the company to achieve its objectives while avoiding unnecessary conflicts. Shareholders, board members, consumers, and the many communities inside an enterprise (Executive Management, Operations, Project Management, Process Improvement, Information Technology, and so on) all have different demands that must be balanced. When done well, governance fosters an open, honest atmosphere that supports structure in planning and execution and encourages board members and executive committees to invest in the corporation's ability to innovate and expand. The decent behaviour and sound judgement of individuals in charge of operating an organization are crucial to successful governance. The corporate governance framework is made up of explicit and implicit contracts between the company and stakeholders for the distribution of responsibilities, rights, and rewards; procedures for resolving stakeholders' sometimes conflicting interests based on their duties, privileges, and roles; and procedures for proper supervision, control, and information-flows to serve as a system of checks and balances. It has to do with the corporate structure's complexity, notably the growth of group entities like subsidiaries, associates, joint ventures, and special-purpose corporations, which are typically piled on top of one another. Boards of Directors of group entities below the parent frequently have relatively limited governance responsibilities, and these entities are often out of the sight of the group Board of Directors and senior management. The author tells you how companies and regulators must concentrate on group governance concerns as well as the governance and management of supply chain business partners.

The management of a corporation's relationships with its management, Board of Directors, shareholders, and other stakeholders The provision of a framework through which the company's objectives are established, as well as the monitoring of the tools employed to achieve these objectives, including performance monitoring in this respect, increases the openness of the company's decision-making processes. The provision of appropriate incentives for the Board of Directors and management to achieve goals that are in the best interests of the corporation and its shareholders. Risk management and the reduction of the consequences of commercial misadventure is a large part of how a corporation is governed and controlled, which is determined by its ownership structure.

Corporate Governance Philosophy In India

As a good corporate citizen, the Company is devoted to sound business practises based on conscience, transparency, fairness, professionalism, and responsibility in order to develop the trust of its many stakeholders in it and pave the path for its long-term success. Friedman correctly stated, *"Corporate governance is to operate the business in line with the owner or shareholder's objective, which is normally to earn as much money as possible while conforming to the basic principles of society incorporated into legislation and local customs."*

Good governance practises are influenced by the organization's culture and attitude, as well as the individuals in control. Corporate governance is a value-based framework for doing business in a fair and transparent manner. In all of its transactions, it assures accountability, openness, and justice, and it satisfies the expectations of all stakeholders. Diverse components should be communicated to various stakeholders in a timely and accurate manner. Corporate governance is the practise of adhering to ethical norms for successful wealth management and distribution, as well as accepting social responsibility for the long-term growth of all stakeholders, including consumers, workers, and society as a whole. Corporate governance is the set of processes, practises, policies, rules, regulations, and laws that regulate how corporations are conducted in the best interests of their stakeholders. Corporate governance is concerned with respecting the law's spirit rather than merely the text. Corporate governance standards should go above and beyond what is required by law. Corporate governance refers to the act of communicating honestly and transparently to the outside world about how the organisation operates on the inside. By delegating decision-making to appropriate management levels, corporate governance creates checks and balances in decision-making. Corporate governance, in other words, should be an integrated component of the decision-making process. Corporate governance can be accomplished through the use of best legal and managerial practices, ethics, wealth creation management, and foresight.Corporate governance is an important instrument for protecting and maximising the long-term wealth of shareholders. Thus, corporate governance can be defined as an approach in which corporations are managed in an ethical, accountable, transparent, and fair manner, with a blend of legal and management practises to imbed the same in the decision-making process of a company and to communicate the same accurately and timely, in such a way that both stakeholders' expectations and legal standards are not only met, but the corporations try to exceed them.

Indian Companies' Corporate Governance Philosophy

- Corporate governance is a collection of procedures and practises that guarantee that a company's affairs are handled in a way that promotes accountability, transparency, and fairness in all of its transactions in the broadest sense and meets its stakeholders' ambitions and societal expectations. Corporate governance is a journey for continuously improving sustainable value creation and is an upward moving target. It requires professionals to raise their competency and capability levels to meet the expectations of managing the enterprise and its resources effectively with the highest standards of ethics.
- Corporate governance is a system of procedures, practises, policies, rules, regulations, and laws by which corporations are directed, managed, and administered by management in the best interests of stakeholders. It ensures the fairness, openness, accountability, and integrity of management. Corporate governance is more of a way of life than a legal requirement. is more of a manner of life than a legal requirement. Corporate governance is the application of ethical norms to the successful management and distribution of wealth, as well as the fulfilment

of social duty for the long-term development of all stakeholders, including consumers, workers, and society. Corporate governance is the strict adherence to the text and spirit of the law, rules, and regulations. Corporate governance establishes clear benchmarks against which responsibility's performance can be assessed.

- Corporate governance is a comprehensive mechanism that directs and controls firms in order to improve their wealth-generating ability. Because major corporations consume a significant amount of social resources, the governance process should ensure that these resources are used in a way that meets the goals of stakeholders and society's expectations.Any genuine corporate governance policy must empower the company's top management. At the same time, governance must establish a system of checks and balances to guarantee that the executive management's decision-making abilities are used with care and responsibility in order to satisfy stakeholders' ambitions and social expectations. Trusteeship, openness, empowerment, responsibility, control, and ethical corporate citizenship are the foundations of corporate governance philosophy.
- Company governance aids in the achievement of corporate goals by establishing a framework within which stakeholders may most effectively pursue the organization's goals. Corporate governance refers to management's acknowledgement of shareholders' inalienable rights as the genuine owners of the company, as well as their own position as trustees on their behalf. Corporate governance ensures principles, ethical corporate practises, openness, and disclosures in accordance with legal regulations and norms.
- Good corporate governance practises are defined by an organization's solid commitment to and implementation of ethical procedures in all of its dealings with a diverse collection of stakeholders. Corporate governance extends beyond legal requirements and is rooted in fundamental corporate principles and values that must be followed in word and spirit. Good

corporate governance standards are also necessary for a long-term business strategy that generates value for all of the company's stakeholders. It is focused on the implementation of open procedures and approaches. It is concerned about the high levels of disclosure required for disseminating corporate, financial, and operational information to all stakeholders. Corporate governance is concerned with establishing a well-defined corporate structure with checks and balances and delegating decision-making to appropriate levels of management.

- Corporate governance is a value-based framework for doing business in a fair and transparent manner. The goal of the corporate governance framework is to provide responsibility in all aspects of business and to use democratic and open methods. Corporate governance is concerned with upholding the spirit of the law rather than the letter of the law. Corporate governance standards should go above and beyond what is required by law. Transparency is important to Corporate Governance, thus it maintains a high level of information. Corporate governance entails communicating the company's internal operations to the public in an open and honest way. Management is the trustee, not the owner, of the capital of the shareholders.
- Compliance with legal and regulatory standards is just part of good company governance. Good governance enables the bank to more effectively manage and oversee its operations, as well as maintain a high level of corporate ethics and maximise value for all of its stakeholders.The goal of corporate governance is to protect and enhance shareholder value, as well as the interests of other stakeholders such as customers, employees, and society at large, to ensure transparency and integrity in communication and to make full, accurate, and clear information available to all parties involved, to ensure accountability for performance and customer service, and to achieve excellence at all levels, and to provide corporate leadership. Establishing properly written and transparent management procedures for policy creation,

implementation, review, decision-making, monitoring, control, and reporting are all part of corporate governance.

- Corporate governance is a critical component of increasing efficiency, growth, and investor trust. As a good corporate citizen, the company should be committed to sound corporate practises based on awareness, openness, fairness, professionalism, and accountability in order to gain the trust of its many stakeholders and pave the way for long-term success.
- Going beyond the letter of the law in sustaining corporate governance standards; Maintaining openness and a high level of disclosure Making a distinct distinction between personal convenience and business resources;Communicating internally in a genuine way maintaining a basic and transparent corporate structure that is exclusively driven by business demands in all countries where the firm operates; Adopting a trusteeship model in which management, rather than being the owner, is the trustee of the shareholders' money.

"Corporate governance is concerned with holding the balance between economic and social goals and between individual and communal goals. The governance framework is there to encourage the efficient use of resources and equally to require accountability for the stewardship of those resources. The aim is to align as nearly as possible the interests of individuals, corporations and society."
(Sir Adrian Cadbury, UK, Commission Report: Corporate Governance 1992)

Operational Ambit

In today's globalized financial markets, this is extremely important. Companies may borrow money from a much bigger pool of investors because of international capital flows. Corporate governance structures must be trustworthy, widely understood across borders, and adhere to globally accepted norms if enterprises and governments are to realise the full benefits of the global capital market and attract long-term capital. Even if corporations do not primarily rely on foreign sources of capital, a credible corporate governance framework backed by effective supervision and enforcement mechanisms will help boost domestic investor confidence, lower capital costs, support the smooth operation of financial markets, and ultimately attract more stable sources of funding.The corporate governance structure should encourage open and fair markets as well as efficient resource allocation. It should adhere to the rule of law and promote effective oversight and enforcement. Effective corporate governance necessitates a stable legal, regulatory, and institutional framework on which market actors may depend when forming private contractual relationships. This corporate governance framework usually consists of aspects of legislation, regulation, self-regulatory frameworks, voluntary pledges, and company practises that are based on a country's unique circumstances, history, and tradition. As a result, the ideal balance of law, regulation, self-regulation, volunteer norms, and other factors will differ from country to country. Soft law aspects based on the *"comply or explain"* concept, such as corporate governance codes, can be productively supplemented by legislative and regulatory parts of the corporate governance framework to allow for flexibility and address the specificities of individual organizations. What works effectively in one firm, for one investor, or for one stakeholder may not be relevant to other corporations, investors, or stakeholders operating in a different environment and under different conditions. The various aspects of the corporate governance framework should be examined and, if required, updated when new experiences and business conditions arise. Proper governance takes time and consideration from dedicated leaders who see the value of coordinating all levels of a business to achieve desired outcomes. More than ever, board members and other corporate executives must be prepared to deal with unprecedented levels of uncertainty.The global economic landscape is evolving as a result of increased globalisation, technological proliferation, and the increased urgency around climate change and biodiversity loss. In the face of the COVID-19 epidemic, board members and other corporate executives are obligated to confront these issues. Without a doubt, the negative consequences of these complicated events signal that a major overhaul of corporate governance is not just essential, but also demanded – and business executives must be ready.

Corporate governance guarantees that a company's environment is fair and transparent, and that workers may be held responsible for their activities. Poor corporate governance, on the other hand, leads to waste, mismanagement, and corruption. Only excellent governance can ensure lasting and reliable commercial performance, regardless of the type of endeavour. Accountability, fairness, openness, assurance, leadership, and stakeholder management are the cornerstones of good corporate governance. All six are necessary for a company's performance and the development of strong professional relationships with its stakeholders, which include board members, managers, workers, customers, regulators, and, most significantly, shareholders.

- Corporate governance is balancing the interests of a company's many stakeholders, including shareholders, management, customers, suppliers, financiers, the government, and the general public.
- It provides proper transparency and effective decision-making in order to meet company objectives.
- Compliance with regulations and laws is aided by corporate governance.
- It promotes greater transparency in commercial transactions.
- It ensures that ideals are upheld and that business is conducted in an ethical manner.
- At the head of affairs, a governing body capable of making independent and impartial judgments is in place.
- The govening body oversees non-executive and independent Directors in order to protect shareholders‘ interests.
- The governing body follows open procedures and bases its decisions on accurate and complete data.

- It has influence over important changes that affect the firm.
- Governing body successfully controls and monitors the company's affairs as well as the management team's activities.

Advantages Of Excellent Corporate Governance:

- It builds morale, a reputation, and a legacy. Putting in place procedures that promote good governance strengthens a company's identity, allowing stakeholders and potential investors to place greater faith in it, allowing you to form better long-term partnerships.
- It increases the financial performance success rate and improves sustainability.
- It increases the capacity to recruit and retain talent. A lot of emphasis has been placed on culture as a major contributor to a company's success. Maintaining openness in areas such as fairness, accountability, and operations provides your staff with a better feeling of responsibility and knowledge of their role in creating value inside the company.
- It creates an efficient framework for achieving corporate goals and Major stakeholders such as workers, suppliers, and the community have all been considered in decision-making, resulting in a broader vision for successful outcomes. Providing each stakeholder with a proportion of useful engagement fosters a more responsible culture, increasing the likelihood of achieving organizational goals.
- It increases your chances of gaining a competitive advantage. It creates investment opportunities. An organization that symbolizes stability and dependability has a higher chance of attracting premium investors as well as a better chance of borrowing money at a lower cost.
- It provides a practical framework for all stages of decision-making: The capacity to make well-informed judgments may boost productivity and mitigate the consequences of future errors. Ensuring that information is easily available to important

stakeholders, i.e., a culture of transparency, is one strategy to encourage this type of decision-making skill.

- Strong corporate governance standards may improve the effectiveness and efficiency of business operations by instilling values throughout the organization, which has the potential to generate significant advantages.
- It creates investment opportunities. An organization that symbolises stability and dependability has a higher chance of attracting premium investors as well as a better chance of borrowing money at a lower cost.
- It provides a practical framework for all stages of decision-making. The capacity to make well-informed judgments may boost productivity and mitigate the consequences of future errors. Ensuring that information is easily available to important stakeholders, i.e., a culture of transparency, is one strategy to encourage this type of decision-making skill.

Corporate governance, as the name indicates, relates to how a business chooses to govern itself, and it is underpinned by a system of rules that provide direction and control in order to achieve its objectives. The continuous implementation of these rules and principles strives to build a healthy, compliant, transparent, and accountable corporate culture that is regularly examined and developed in order to guarantee that your behaviour matches the values your company aspires to reflect, among other things. The deployment of a strong governance protocol is designed to help with the capacity to swiftly detect concerns and make quick choices to remedy them, hence lowering the chance of a crisis and the expenses associated with it. Every industry is continually developing or has the potential to do so in the future. It is vital to ensure that your organization is adaptive to change and that you create an atmosphere where your practises can be perpetuated if you want to maintain a competitive edge and a chance of survival. Corporations require robust governance frameworks that provide them with the tools they need to mitigate risk and make sound choices. Board members, steering executives, and managers should all understand their duties and how they fit into the larger organizational structure once a firm has established its governance guidelines. Each person's role is solidified via governance, ensuring that they do not stray from the purpose. Proper governance structures explain the rules and methods for making corporate decisions, as well as the allocation of rights and obligations among different members in the business.

"A company without governance is like a railway without a track. No matter how much potential the company has, it will never go through the necessary business transformation to get to where it wants to go since it has nothing to guide it."

Wilful Blindness

You have seen several examples of poor governance procedures leading to considerable market value depreciation throughout history. You witnessed it in 2001, when Enron was wiped out by a well-publicised accounting scam. You saw it again in 2014, when GM's inability to heed a whistleblower's warnings about its faulty ignition switches resulted in fines, penalties, and settlements totaling more than $2 billion. Wells Fargo workers, customers, and shareholders have lately been impacted by investigations into aggressive product cross-selling practises and misleading brokerage clients about trading high-fee debt products. So, what makes a corporate governance programme effective in terms of increasing a company's chances of success rather than failure? A lack of corporate governance may result in economic loss, corruption, and a damaged image, not only for the company, but for society as a whole, or even worse, for the entire world. This type of corporate governance is also intended to reduce risk and eliminate corrosive components inside a company. Education, tighter accounting controls, corporate governance, transparency, and disclosure are some of the areas of improvement and ways countries can maintain their leading position in the financial markets so that minorities and foreign countries can invest and exercise greater oversight over corporations.

According to the story, two weavers offer an emperor a new suit of clothing that is invisible to people who are unsuited for their positions, ignorant, or inept. No one dares to declare they don't see any suit of clothing on the emperor as he parades before his subjects in his new attire for fear of being labelled *"unfit for their positions, ignorant, or inept." "But he isn't wearing anything at all!"* a youngster finally exclaims. Everyone begins to laugh and point to the naked monarch. It also makes statutory disclosures and notifies any parties who may be impacted by its decisions. You may not realize the significance of this child's story until many years later. It describes how boards of Directors, executive management teams, and other commercial groupings, although made up of mostly good people, can operate fraudulently or corruptly.

Unfortunately, corporate governance did not receive much attention until the Sarbanes-Oxley Act was enacted into law by President Bush in 2002. The Act included a slew of changes aimed at enhancing corporate accountability and preventing financial fraud. Changes imposed by the Act may not have seemed significant at the time, but extensive fraud that bankrupted Enron and WorldCom caused significant market upheaval. Whether we're talking about trading, financial, corruption, environmental, or safety-related scandals, they frequently arise in companies with corporate cultures that prioritise profits over ethics, safety, or the environment. With the right corporate culture, the Deepwater Horizon environmental disaster, Takata's airbag failure, Tepco's nuclear power plant disaster, GM's ignition switch failure, Olympus and Toshiba's accounting scandals, Volkwagen's emissions scandal, and GlaxoSmithKline's and Leighton Holdings' bribery scandals would not have happened. Many investors were concerned that if firms continued to mismanage their assets and investments, they would lose money. The Sarbanes-Oxley Act gave investors a sense of security. Proper governance, on the other hand, is no longer only about investor protection; it is now a must for firms to prosper. Project management and company reform efforts fail more frequently without adequate governance, making potential investors hesitant. According to the Enron story, every time you turn a stone, another worm emerges. That appears to be the tale of the Enron scandal. Not a day goes by without a fresh revelation of corporate wrongdoing, and one begins to question if there is anything in our enterprise's protocols and structure that can avoid such a disaster. Enron is a good illustration of how individuals at the top permitted a culture of secrecy, rule-breaking, and fraudulent behaviour to thrive. It also had a task group for corporate social responsibility and a code of conduct in the areas of security, human rights, social investment, and public participation. Despite this, no one obeyed the rules. The Board of Directors openly permitted management to violate the code, particularly when the CFO was permitted to serve on special-purpose entities (SPEs); the audit committee permitted suspect accounting practises while making no attempt to investigate SPE transactions; and the auditors failed to prevent questionable accounting. It has co-filed a shareholder petition in response to concerns that Wal-Mart Stores Inc., the US supermarket conglomerate, is not adhering to its own corporate governance requirements. Karina Litvack is the Director of governance and long-term investment. Despite having robust rules on paper, Wal-Mart has had difficulty implementing them across its US operations. As a consequence of the company's unwillingness to engage in a fruitful debate about how it develops and promotes a compliance culture, they have joined a worldwide coalition of significant filers led by the New York City Employees' Retirement System in filing a shareholder proposal. What might be the cause of such a massive collapse? It's one of corporate India's worst unfolding chapters. The organization's top-level management underestimated the severity of the gangrene. The function of the auditors is also being questioned, as is how such a large-scale financial wrongdoing could have gone undiscovered. A business will always have two sides; it is not required to make profits all of the time, but it is vital to maintain the integrity of the firm. Workplace stress can reduce a company's productivity.

Efficiency will suffer if leadership is poisonous.The leadership and governance given by those at the top will have a big impact on how well these risks are managed. Enron, FIFA, and The News of the World are just a few instances of companies where poor leadership contributed to widespread unethical behaviour. When things go wrong, however, top leaders nearly always find it incredibly difficult to detouch themselves. It's not every day that a job advertisement catches the attention of the press. Every day, a merger or acquisition takes place somewhere. However, owing to Satyam's projected image, co-players in the market are abandoning their ambitions to acquire the company. If the industry can rebuild the faith of the same investors that Satyam duped, the company's corporate governance failure may encourage competitors to pursue market share generated by its aftermath.

The Statutory Part Of Corporate Governance

The higher the degree of corporate governance, the more powerful the corporation is from the perspective of its shareholders. The active and independent Directors are the ones who inject and contribute to portraying the company as one with a good perspective. Corporate governance laws in India compel corporations to audit their working culture and provide a more favourable picture to the shareholder community since their activities have several legal ramifications. The new rules, which came into effect after the Companies Act of 2013, are highly balanced. Shareholders are involved in company decision-making, and numerous protections have been implemented to ensure that the interests of shareholders and society as a whole are not overlooked.Corporate governance fosters the much-needed openness in businesses.As a result, it propels India forward in the global race of growing economies.

Corporate governance is dependent on the integrity and effectiveness of the financial markets. Poor corporate governance limits a company's potential and can result in financial difficulties and fraud. Companies with good governance outperform their competition and attract investors who can help fund future growth.

The Principles of Corporate Governance, issued by the Organization for Economic Cooperation and Development in 1999, have since become a global benchmark for governments, investors, corporations, and other stakeholders. They've also been adopted as one of the Financial Stability Board's Key Standards for Sound Financial Systems, and they serve as the basis for the World Bank's Corporate Governance Reports on Standards and Codes Compliance (ROSC).On April 22, 2004, the OECD announced an updated version of the OECD Principles of Corporate Governance. It includes a lot of new ideas as well as revisions to old ones. Members of the OECD and representatives from OECD and non-OECD countries participated in a consultation process. The OECD's regional corporate governance roundtables in Latin America, Asia, the Middle East, and North Africa, as well as experts, an online public consultation, and the OECD's official advisory bodies, the Business and Industry Advisory Committee (BIAC) and the Trade Union Advisory Committee, conducted a second review of the principles in 2014/15, based on the 2004 version of the principles (TUAC). Businesses should ensure that they have systems in place to resolve any possible conflicts of interest and offer a framework for internal complaints regarding management or board appointments, according to the OECD guidelines. A company's management, Board of Directors, shareholders, and other stakeholders are all involved in corporate governance. Corporate governance also establishes the framework within which the company's goals are created, as well as the methods for achieving those goals and measuring success. The principles are meant to be simple, easy to grasp, and accessible to the international community. The role of government, semi- government, and private sector initiatives is to assess the quality of the corporate governance framework and develop more detailed mandatory or voluntary provisions that can take into account country-specific economic, legal, and cultural differences based on the principles. The Principles apply to both financial and non-financial publicly traded firms. They may also be a valuable instrument for improving corporate governance in firms whose shares are not publicly traded, to the degree that they are judged suitable. While some of the principles may be more applicable to bigger organizations than to smaller businesses, regulators may aim to enhance awareness of good corporate governance. Individual market participants, board members, and firm leaders' business judgments are not to be influenced or second-guessed by the Principles. What works in one firm or for one set of investors may not be relevant to all businesses or to issues of systemic economic significance. Employees' and other stakeholders' interests are recognized in the Principles, as well as their critical role in the company's long-term growth and performance. Other relevant factors to a company's decision-making processes, such as environmental, anti-corruption, or ethical concerns, are considered in the Principles but are addressed more explicitly in a number of other instruments, such as the OECD Guidelines for Multinational Enterprises, the Convention on Combating Bribery of Foreign Public Officials in International Business Transactions, and the United Nations Convention on the Elimination of Racial Discrimination in International Business Transactions. Other relevant factors to a company's decision-making processes, such as environmental, anti-corruption, or ethical concerns, are addressed more explicitly in a number of other instruments, such as the OECD Guidelines for Multinational Enterprises, the Convention on Combating Bribery of Foreign Public Officials in International Business Transactions, the UN Guiding Principles on Business and Human Rights, and the ILO Declaration on Fund Management.

The board's responsibilities are described in the OECD Principles of Corporate Governance (2004), and some of them are summarized below.

- Board members should be well-informed and act in the company's and shareholders' best interests by acting ethically and in good faith, with due diligence and care.

- Corporate strategy, goal-setting, key action plans, risk management, capital plans, and yearly budgets are all evaluated and directed in charge of overseeing significant purchases and divestitures.
- Key executives are chosen, compensated, monitored, and replaced, and succession planning is overseen.
- Align key executive and board remuneration (pay) with the company's and shareholders' long-term objectives.
- Ensure a proper and transparent nomination and election procedure for board members.
- Ensure the integrity of the company's accounting and financial reporting systems, as well as their independent auditing.
- Ascertain that adequate internal control systems are in place.
- Oversee the disclosure and communication processes.
- Where board committees are formed, their mandate, composition, and working processes should be clearly defined and made public.

Certain governance criteria must be met by companies listed on the New York Stock Exchange (NYSE) and other stock exchanges. The NYSE Listed Company Manual, for example, requires, among other things, Directors who are self-employed: "A majority of independent Directors is required for listed businesses... In carrying out their tasks, effective boards of Directors use independent judgement. The need for a majority of independent Directors would improve board supervision and reduce the risk of serious conflicts of interest." Section 303A.01 (Section 303A.01.)An independent Director is not employed by the firm and does not have a "material financial connection" with it. In order to enable non-management Directors to act as a more effective check on management, each listed company's non-management Directors must meet at regularly scheduled executive sessions without management. Section 303A.03 (Section 303A.03). According to their charters, boards organise their members into committees with distinct functions. A nominating/corporate governance committee made up completely of independent Directors is required for publicly traded businesses. This committee is in charge of nominating new board members. Compensation and Audit Committees are also mentioned, with the latter subject to a number of listing rules as well as external restrictions.

Keeping that concept in mind, the following are the basic components of good corporate governance:

1. The Director's autonomy and effectiveness:

The Board of Directors is responsible for a variety of responsibilities, including: Appointing and managing the Chief Executive Officer, as well as establishing a long-term strategic vision. A majority of independent Directors on the most effective boards are able to monitor corporate management and independent committees for the interests of shareholders. These Directors should be present at the meetings and ready to debate important topics. Long-serving Directors may get too enmeshed in their organizations to be regarded as fully independent. The habit of board members *"overboarding"* should likewise be a source of worry. This refers to circumstances in which Directors serve on the boards of too many different publicly listed firms or nonprofit organizations to be successful. As a result, these Directors may find themselves unable to attend meetings, prepare questions, address important problems, or provide proper service to the shareholders who elected them. Typically, the chairperson of the Board of Directors and the CEO of a firm should be appointed independently. However, if there is an independent leadership position on the board, such as a lead Director to offer a counterweight, it may be suitable to combine the responsibilities. Otherwise, the combined CEO and chair may exert undue influence over the board, causing a conflict of interest. Allowing a CEO to create a loan with unsuitable or self-serving terms is an example of this sort of conflict. Perhaps the Directors should have seen the problems earlier and adopted a different approach? The structures and methods for the direction and management of businesses are referred to as corporate governance.It also involves the management, the Board of Directors, controlling shareholders, minority shareholders, and other stakeholders' interactions. Openness to public disclosure, high transparency, and accountability are essential characteristics of good corporate governance that promote the long-term viability of businesses and society. Good corporate governance is required to avoid mismanagement by allowing organizations to function more effectively, enhance access to capital, limit risk, and protect stakeholders. It also makes businesses more responsible and transparent to investors, reducing the risk of expropriation and injustice to shareholders. In order to prevent frequent boardroom prejudices, prospective board members should be able to not only express their own opinions but also actively engage with the perspectives of others. According to the poll results, a future-ready board member is honest and specific in their questions and is wary of accepting answers at face value. Board members should also be truthful in their efforts to bring all aspects of diversity to the table, as well as a perspective that may not have existed previously. Each board position must be filled by someone who has a global citizen attitude and is dedicated to taking steps to improve diversity, equity, and inclusion.

2. A focus on diversity:

According to studies, companies with more varied boards of Directors are more risk averse, have less volatile stock returns, and are more likely to pay dividends. As a result, it may be argued that a primary aim for the makeup of any company's board and senior management ranks should be diversity by gender, age, and minority participation.

3.Management and evaluation of compensation on a regular basis:

The evaluation and monitoring of remuneration at both the board and top management levels is another important aspect of corporate governance. Typically, the chairperson of the Board of Directors and the CEO of a firm should be appointed independently. However, if there is an independent leadership position on the board, such as a lead Director to offer a counterweight, it may be suitable to combine the responsibilities. Otherwise, the combined CEO and chair may exert undue influence over the board, causing a conflict of interest. Allowing a CEO to create a loan with unsuitable or self-serving terms is an example of this sort of conflict. Pay should be linked to performance, with a focus on long-term goals. By avoiding guaranteed compensation and expensive severance packages, you may avoid *"paying for failure."* For effective supervision, establish an independent pay committee. Ensure that compensation disclosures are transparent and complete. Pay non-executive Directors and keep track of their compensation. Nonexecutive Directors who are overpaid may not be able to make impartial decisions about managers' pay and performance.

4. Transparency and independence of auditors:

A study of auditing methods and financial reporting might potentially flag impending concerns. Auditors should be impartial (with no financial stake in a corporation) and make the majority of their money from auditing rather than consulting. Accounting difficulties should be handled in a transparent manner, with comprehensive, thorough information and reports available to the board at all times, and safeguards in place to avoid a recurrence of any dubious findings. Auditing strengthens the trustworthiness of any company's financial reporting. The auditing process guarantees that financial accounts are accurate and full, making them more reliable and valuable for investment choices. Along with the idea that ownership structure matters in corporate governance, there's also the idea that the company's financial structure, or the ratio of debt to equity, has an impact on governance quality. The level of corporate governance is largely determined by the legal, regulatory, and political context in which a firm works. Corporate governance processes are, in reality, economic and legal entities that are frequently the result of political decisions. For example, the extent to which shareholders can exert control over management is determined by their voting rights as defined by company law, and the extent to which creditors can exercise financial claims against a bankrupt unit is determined by bankruptcy laws and procedures, among other factors.

5. Takeover provisions and shareholder rights:

Shareholder rights should also be considered a vital component of effective governance by investors. Multiple shares/classes are not always indicative of weak governance, but they are something to think about. For example, in the information technology industry, it is customary for firm founders and insiders to own shares with more voting rights than outside investors. Is it possible for shareholders to put suggestions on proxy ballots or nominate Directors? What activities, such as modifying the company's bylaws, may a board conduct without shareholder approval? Are there any measures in place to make it difficult for a firm to be bought, such as poison pills? How is management compensated in the case of a takeover? Shareholder recognition, which is a policy that guarantees that all shareholders have a vote in a company's inner workings, is one of the principles of corporate governance. The value of a company's shares is also secured by shareholder recognition. To ensure that everyone has the same vision of the company's future, the rules and duties of board members must be clearly defined. Stakeholder interest is concerned with the needs of those who are not stockholders. As a result of reaching out to non-members, greater communication and ties with the press and the community are fostered. Corporate governance ethical rules are also critical for ensuring increased profits and keeping the organization out of legal difficulties. Employees and board members are also subject to these restrictions. Transparency must be visible, and it should be.

6. Shareholder influence and proxy voting:

Investors are increasingly using proxy voting to impact a board's corporate supervision and commitment to improving governance on problems including climate change, income inequality, and shareholder proxy access. Shareholders must be able to send a message to the Board of Directors by withholding votes for

Directors if the firm has failed to act on winning shareholder motions, failed to deal with a Director's poor performance, or failed to strengthen board accountability and supervision. Those in charge of governance should identify important stakeholders and how they interact with the business, as well as how they are engaged, in order to secure the best possible outcome for the company. The yearly agenda and strategy plan incorporate stakeholder interaction.

Refinitiv's corporate governance top 100

Explore the full list of the companies leading in corporate governance as of February 2021

1. *Royal Dutch Shell PLC(Netherland) Energy Fossil Fuel Industry*
2. *NK Rosneft' PAO (Russia) Energy Fossil Fuel Industry*
3. *Johnson Matthey (UK) Chemicals Industry*
4. *Endeavour Mining Corp (UK) Mineral Resources*
5. *AIA Group LTD. (HongKong) Indurance*
6. *BHP Group LTD (Australia) Mineral Resources*
7. *Alcoa Corp. (USA) Mineral Resources*
8. *Newmont Corp.(USA) Mineral Resources*
9. *Sime Darby Plantation Bhd. (Malaysia) Food & Beverages*
10. *AngloGold Ashanti LTD. (South Africa) Mineral Resources*
11. *Lundin Energy AB (Sweden) Energy- Fossil Fuel*
12. *SAP SE (Germany) Software & IT Services*
13. *South 32 LTD. (Australia) Mineral Resources*
14. *Allianz SE (Germany) Insurance*
15. *Petra Diamonds LTD. (UK)*
16. *Banco Santander Brasil SA (Brazil) Banking & Investment*
17. *Aenza SAA (Peru) Industrial & Commercial Services*
18. *Mediclinic International PLC (UK) Healthcare & Equipment*
19. *Sony Corp. (Japan) Technology Equipment*
20. *Tanger factory Outlet Centers INC. (USA) Real Estate*

Corporate Cuture: The Backbone

Corporate culture is defined as a mix of the beliefs, attitudes, and behaviours expressed by a corporation in its operations and relationships with its stakeholders. While corporate governance regulations and standards have improved compliance and the adoption of best practises, they have had far less success in transforming business cultures. Despite considerable reform initiatives and improved knowledge of corporate governance over the last two decades or more, governance failures appear to be on the rise. History often appears to repeat itself. In most other nations across the world where there is concentrated ownership, independent Directors are often appointed by controlling shareholders and are often accountable to these shareholders. Not unexpectedly, they have frequently failed to play a role in questioning choices that are not always in the company's or all shareholders' best interests. According to the author, the notion of independent Directors may fall out of favour and cease to be a credible instrument for guaranteeing effective corporate governance. In reality, in many nations, severe reservations about the usefulness of independent Directors have already been airborne. As we've previously mentioned, the formation of corporate regulation is frequently tied to perceived failures of firms and their management to perform as society expects. This trend is not unique to corporate governance, and, like with accounting, various nations may face challenges at different periods. Some of the most well remembered examples of corporate governance failure are addressed.

"Organizations need to practice qualitative corporate governance rather than quantitative governance thereby ensuring it is properly run." – and "You cannot legislate good behaviour." – Mervyn King

The 2022 World's Most Ethical Companies Honoree List

"In 2022, 136 organizations are recognized for their unwavering commitment to business integrity. The honorees span 22 countries and 45 industries, and include 14 first-time honorees and 6 organizations that have been named to the honoree list 16 times, marking every year since its inception."

1. *3M Industrial Manufacturing United States*
2. *Accenture Consulting Services Ireland*

3. ADM Food, Beverage & Agriculture United States
4. AECOM Engineering Services United States
5. Alfac Incor. Accident & Life Insurance United States
6. Allianz Life Accident & Life Insurance United States
7. Apple Technology United States
8. Aptiv PLC Automotive Ireland
9. ARM Semiconductors United Kingdom
10. AT&T Telecomm United States
11. Avangrid Energy & Utilities United States
12. Avista Energy & Utilities United States
13. Baptist Health Healthcare Providers United States
14. Best Buy Co. Retail United states
15. Blue Shield Health insurance California
16. BMO Fin Gr. Banks Canada
17. Booz Allen Hamilton Consultation United States
18. Brown- Forman Food- Beverage United States
19. Cambia Health Health Insurance United States
20. Canon U.S.A Imaging Technology United States
21. Capgemini Consultation France
22. Capital Power Energy & Utilities Canada
23. Carefirst Health Insurance United States
24. CBRE Real States United States
25. Cementos Argos Construction Colombia

"Corporate governance is the system by which companies are directed and controlled. It encompasses the entire mechanics of the functioning of a company and attempt to put in place a system of checks and balances between the shareholders, Directors, employees, auditor and the management." Cadbury Committee (U.K.), 1992

The Principles of Good Governance

Corporate governance's principal purpose is to increase long-term shareholder value while also safeguarding the interests of other stakeholders. Good corporate governance is essential not just for gaining credibility and trust, but also for survival, expansion, and consolidation as part of strategic management. Organizations that want to strengthen governance should examine their internal business structures, procedures, and initiatives closely. When it comes to determining what defines effective governance, the 10 principles listed below are a good place to start:

- Individual responsibilities, organizational expectations of leaders, and the functions of the executive and steering committees should all be clearly defined.
- An executive committee must be composed of the correct individuals, with special attention paid to each individual's background, talents, and experience, as well as how the addition of one person enhances the committee's collective potential and successful functioning.
- The executive committee is responsible for establishing the organization's vision, purpose, and strategy, as well as assisting the organization in understanding them and adjusting plans to put them into action. Executive committees may assist in raising the possibility that their firms will deliver on their goal by putting in place an effective system of risk supervision and internal controls.
- It is critical that the executive committee ensures that information flows to the board that aids decision-making; that there is transparency and accountability to external stakeholders and employees throughout the organization; and that the integrity of financial statements and other key information is protected.
- The executive committee has a responsibility to play in improving the organization's capacity and capabilities.
- The executive committee assists a company in efficiently engaging with stakeholders and workers. Accountability entails taking responsibility for the strategy and tasks necessary to achieve organizational objectives. This applies to all levels of the organization, from employees to senior executives, who embrace risk management within a formalised risk appetite. This includes cultivating a compliance culture in order to

generate a real and perceived belief that the entity is operating within internal and external constraints.

- Treating all stakeholders, particularly minorities, fairly and equally, and providing appropriate remedies for infractions is what fairness entails. It is critical to establish efficient communication mechanisms in order to ensure the equitable and timely protection of resources and human assets, as well as the correction of errors.The coexistence of state-owned, private, and international enterprises is a feature of our business sector. The composition of business boards, like the structure of ownership, has a significant impact on how firms are governed and controlled. The Board of Directors is in charge of setting business goals, formulating broad policies, and appointing senior executives to carry out those goals and policies.
- Transparency means having nothing to conceal, allowing others to observe its procedures and transactions.Transparency is an important aspect of corporate governance since it guarantees that an outside observer may review all of an entity's actions at any time. In order to further transparency, non-direct actors must have trust that executive actors are directing the entity toward a pre-defined goal rather than using it for personal gain, as well as get expert advice on how the applied technique may be improved. Assurance services give objective, expert judgments that help to limit the danger of information leakage the risk that comes from incorrect information.
- Accountability is important. Defining and leading the organization's objectives while adhering to the values and principles that govern how business is conducted.Those in charge of governance are in charge of these critical strategic concerns as well as providing leadership in developing the correct culture to drive the company's performance. The organization will languish without clear direction, policy, and processes and is unlikely to achieve its long-term goals and potential. This should involve leadership and core expertise renewal to ensure knowledge and experience retention, as well

as proper representation and continuity.

- Future-ready board members will have a profound sense of curiosity and a readiness to learn in order to achieve this. They'll be ready to adjust their perspective when they make a concerted attempt to listen to stakeholders who all have different and opposing expectations. They appreciate the interconnectedness of needs and are dedicated to creating solutions that satisfy environmental, stakeholder, and shareholder requirements. Future-ready stewards are collectively directed by a value-driven purpose that promotes health and well-being via proven action in resolving structural disparities in order to construct more equitable, diverse, and prepared businesses. A mission that extends beyond the goal and necessitates a high level of accountability in terms of keeping commitments.

"If people are good only because they fear punishment, and hope for reward, then we are a sorry lot indeed." – Albert Einstein

Creating a Strong Governance Structure

Good governance means that your company's operations are designed to produce outcomes that fulfil societal and organizational needs while making smart use of its resources. Because strong leadership is needed to drive inspiration within an organization, these policies and principles are first practised and influenced by leadership. This is a crucial component of success since it allows for the establishment of growth prospects and a competitive edge. For firms to position themselves favourably in order to weather a challenging economic climate, good corporate governance has become a crucial emphasis area.

Effective governance structures enable firms to produce value via innovation, development, and exploration while also ensuring accountability and control mechanisms that are proportional to the risks they face. A minimal, clear, and unambiguous governance structure is essential. This begins with the formation of an Executive Committee tasked with coordinating all levels of the company to achieve set strategic goals and objectives.The organization and its investment portfolio must be reviewed by members of the Executive Committee. Members of the Executive Committee must assess the organization and its investment portfolio to ensure that plans are on track to achieve their objectives. A genuinely outstanding Executive Committee would also evaluate organizational performance (including procedures and policies) in order to predict future demands and avoid regulatory violations.

Recurring reviews are an important part of effective governance. Sub-committees must assess performance in order to determine if project, process, system, departmental, or data improvements have met their objectives. They will be required to offer improvements or ideas that would enhance procedures and systems in many circumstances. The Executive Committee can then evaluate these recommendations to see if they want to support these courses and spend money on them, or if they want to develop other plans or objectives for progress. If the organization's strategic plan has to be updated, the Executive Committee is the one who makes the modifications.

Final Touch

In conclusion, the responsibility that an individual assumes when charged with the governance of an entity is significant, and it should only be undertaken with a clear understanding of, and commitment to, fulfilling this responsibility to the best of their ability, first and foremost for the benefit of the stakeholders. Individual and organizational performance will both benefit from a firm grasp of the concepts and practises of good governance, so how do you and your company do against this checklist? Organizations can benefit from good governance in a variety of ways, including strategies and plans that are better; efficiencies and effectiveness of operations and processes have improved; project management and delivery have improved; compliance with regulatory requirements, as well as financial and risk management, has become more conservative; improved communication and engagement among members and stakeholders/employees;

enhanced agility with which a company can carry out its mission and objectives.

Summing Up

Corporate governance refers to how a corporation is run to guarantee all of its stakeholders receive a fair share of the company's profits and assets. Good corporate governance entails a company's commitment to operating its operations in a lawful, ethical, and transparent manner. Corporate governance is a system of rules, policies, and processes that guide the Board of Directors and independent committees in their monitoring and management of a firm. Good governance practises are influenced by the organization's culture and attitude, as well as the individuals in control. In today's globalized financial markets, this is extremely important. The ideal balance of law, regulation, self-regulation, volunteer norms, and other factors will differ from country to country. Corporate governance can ensure lasting and reliable commercial performance, regardless of the type of endeavour. A lack of corporate governance may result in economic loss, corruption, and a damaged image. Proper corporate governance is no longer only about investor protection; it is now a must for firms to prosper. Corporate governance laws in India compel corporations to audit their working culture. The higher the degree of corporate governance, the more powerful the corporation is from the perspective of its shareholders. Despite considerable reform initiatives and improved knowledge of corporate governance, governance failures appear to be on the rise. The author argues that good corporate governance has become a crucial emphasis area.

CHAPTER FOUR

CORPORATE SOCIAL RESPONSIBILITIES

Companies' Practises And Policies Are Intended To Have A Positive Influence On The World.

"Corporate Social Responsibility is a hard-edged business decision. Not because it is a nice thing to do or because people are forcing us to do it because it is good for our business" -Niall Fitzerald, Former CEO, Unilever

CSR has been the subject of several discussions and studies over the last few years. It has become more important in both academic and corporate circles. It encompasses a wide range of ideals and criteria for assessing a company's social impact. Many related and overlapping ideas, including corporate citizenship, business ethics, stakeholder management, and sustainability, have evolved as a result of the constant usage of the word *"CSR."* Multiple views and by those in supporting positions such as the business sector, government agencies, academia, and the public sector are indicated by the wide range of synonymously used terminology.

- CSR is a sort of self-regulation practised by businesses with the goal of becoming socially responsible. It enables businesses to assess their influence on all parts of society, including economic, social, and environmental factors.

- CSR refers to a company's decision to operate in ways that benefit society and the environment rather than harm them.
- CSR is a company strategy that promotes long-term growth by providing economic, social, and environmental benefits to all stakeholders.
- CSR is a broad topic with several meanings and applications. Each firm and nation has its own manner of understanding and implementing it.
- Furthermore, CSR is a broad term that encompasses a wide range of issues, including human rights, corporate governance, health and safety, environmental impacts, working conditions, and economic growth.
- CSR refers to a company's activities and policies that benefit the environment, the economy, and society. Customers, suppliers, shareholders, and workers, as well as the government, have their demands met.
- Whatever definition is used, the goal of CSR is to promote change that leads to long-term sustainability.
- CSR refers to how a corporation balances economic, environmental, and social goals while also meeting stakeholder expectations and maintaining or increasing shareholder value.
- CSR refers to a company's total connection with its stakeholders, which includes customers, workers, communities, owners/investors, the government, suppliers, and rivals. Investment in community outreach, employee relations, job development and retention, environmental responsibility, and financial success are all examples of CSR.
- CSR is a term that refers to company actions that help society. CSR can include a range of strategies, such as donating a percentage of a company's profits to charity or establishing *"greener"* business practises. There are a few major areas of social responsibility that many firms today are pursuing.
- CSR is influenced by culture, religion, family values and customs, and industrialization.

- CSR enables both large and small enterprises to have a beneficial impact. It occurs when businesses make the decision to do the right thing not only for their profit line, but also to create consumer trust.

The Principles & Goals Of CSR

The company must follow and comprehend all applicable local, national, and international laws and regulations, as well as all written, stated, and enforced laws and regulations, in line with established, specialised processes. The firm must declare its policies, choices, and operations in a clear, accurate, and complete manner, including any known or possible consequences for the environment and society. The company shall implement policies and procedures that will result in the respect of existing human rights as defined in the Universal Declaration of Human Rights.

The following areas may be recommended to meet some of these goals: Reducing gas emissions and waste, recycling resources, and replanting projects are all examples of environmental protection. Donating to charity and engaging in social causes, such as raising awareness about human rights and contemporary issues, are examples of charitable actions. Urban area development, in collaboration with the government, aims at reviving small businesses and improving the environment in smaller communities. investment in local businesses, in collaboration with non-governmental organizations, in the areas of poverty reduction and social development initiatives. projects that benefit employees, such as establishing greater standards for professional health and safety, providing equitable employment opportunities, and providing flexible work hours. Enterprise activities, operations, and services result in both direct and indirect emissions into the atmosphere. These emissions are caused by the company's goods, as well as its shopping habits and power use. Various pollutants, such as lead, mercury, volatile organic compounds, sulphur dioxide, nitric oxide, and other elements, may be released, resulting in environmental degradation and adverse impacts on human health.

Those businesses whose operations generate liquid and solid waste should rely on waste reduction strategies. Reduced sources, reutilization, recycling, waste treatment, and disposal must all be part of these initiatives.Businesses need energy to conduct their operations and provide services. Programs that focus on efficient power usage in buildings, such as heating, cooling, and lighting, as well as efficient fuel use and dependence on alternative fuel supplies, may reduce the demand for electricity in buildings. Clean water is regarded as a worldwide resource. Obtaining safe drinking water is seen as a basic human necessity, and it is included as one of a person's main rights. The provision of clean drinking water and health services for all people is one of the new millennium's development goals. Effective water management entails allocating water and managing its flow in order to accomplish just and long-term conservation of water resources. CSR is an important part of every business's operations. There are two sorts of corporate social responsibility to take into account. The first entails businesses contributing money and resources to worthy social causes, such as donating money or staff time to organizations. This is the definition that many people think of when they think of corporate responsibility. Another sort of CSR, on the other hand, entails developing a concrete strategy to manufacture items or deliver services that are beneficial to society. Use of safe materials in design and manufacture, corporate environmental initiatives, and other reasons such as job creation and economic growth are all examples of these.To demonstrate a meaningful commitment to a cause, the most successful corporate social responsibility initiatives combine these two forms of CSR. A company that uses sustainable materials in its products, donates financial resources to environmental causes, and allows employees to volunteer at environmental charities on paid time off, for example, is demonstrating a true commitment to the environment that goes beyond any single CSR initiative. The relevance and popularity of social media is one of the reasons why firms should have visible CSR programs. Corporations that wish to safeguard their brand are aware that public opinion is influenced by social media.When a company engages in social responsibility through fundraising or employee giving programs, using social media to publicise these efforts helps to build a positive brand image, and it's a terrific opportunity to connect with your audience on a deeper level that goes beyond your products or services.

"We cannot lose sight of the fundamental challenges facing future generations. It's critical we take urgent action now to care for the planet and future generations. As a company who looks to children as our role models, we are inspired by the millions of kids who have called for more urgent action on climate change." - Niels B Christiansen, LEGO Group CEO

CSR's Aim

Corporate social responsibility aims to enhance communities, the economy, and the environment. CSR, or corporate social responsibility, is a type of self-regulation that represents a company's accountability and commitment to contributing to the well-being of communities and society through a variety of environmental and social factors. CSR is critical to a company's brand impression, consumer, employee, and investor attraction, talent retention, and overall business success. Environmental initiatives, charitable work, ethical labour practises, and volunteer programs are all examples of CSR activities that a firm might employ. This book is for company owners who wish to learn more about the advantages, best practises, and potential pitfalls of implementing or improving CSR activities. Profitability, growth rate, and brand recognition aren't the only factors that determine a company's success. Customers, workers, and other stakeholders in today's world evaluate a firm based on how its operations affect the community, economy, environment, and society as a whole. In other words, if it is concerned with the greater good rather than just the bottom line, corporate social responsibility practises are a means for your company to show its position on the issue. Corporate social responsibility (CSR) is a sort of self-regulation practised by businesses with the goal of social accountability and a positive influence on society. Being environmentally responsible and eco-conscious; fostering equality, diversity, and inclusion in the workplace; treating workers with respect; giving back to the community; and ensuring business decisions are made with CSR in mind are just a few examples of how a firm may embrace CSR.

The environment is a major focus of corporate social responsibility. Businesses of all sizes have a significant carbon impact. Any efforts businesses may make to lower their carbon footprints are seen as beneficial to the firm as well as society as a whole. Businesses can also demonstrate social responsibility by giving to national and local charities. Businesses have a wealth of resources that may be used to support charities and community activities in their communities. Labor practises that are ethical Companies may show their corporate social responsibility by treating employees fairly and ethically. This is especially true for companies that operate in countries whose labour rules differ from those in the United States.

CSR has progressed from voluntary corporate decisions to required requirements at the regional, national, and international levels. Many businesses, on the other hand, prefer to go beyond their legal obligations and incorporate the concept of "doing good" into their business operations. There is no one-size-fits-all approach to CSR, but one thing is certain: for a company's policies to be viewed as authentic, they must be interwoven into its culture and business processes. In today's socially conscious climate, employees and consumers value working for and spending money on companies that promote CSR. They have the ability to recognise corporate hypocrisy. The company fulfil the demands of customers, suppliers, shareholders, and workers, as well as the government, the general public, and the communities in which the company works, without jeopardising future generations' capacity to meet their own needs. A company's willingness to participate in volunteer events reveals a lot about its genuineness. Companies may demonstrate their concern for certain causes and support for specific groups by taking good actions without expecting anything in return. The CSR approach is comprehensive and integrated with the core business strategy for addressing social and environmental consequences of enterprises, as evidenced by the preceding criteria. CSR must include the well-being of all stakeholders, not only the company's shareholders. CSR is made up of a much bigger collection of operations that have strategic commercial benefits in addition to philanthropic initiatives.

A company's values, business mission, and key concerns should all be examined to identify which activities best connect with the company's aims and culture. The company can either undertake the evaluation internally or pay a third party to do so. While general goals such as good health and well-being or gender equality may be applied to almost any business, specialized goals such as life below water or affordable and clean energy may be applicable to certain industries such as water technology or energy suppliers.Companies who have been doing CSR for a long time, with or without the law, only needed to simplify their spending. The issue or necessity for these companies wasn't so much about boosting spending by a factor of ten, but rather about having the opportunity to examine and re-strategize what they were currently doing in order to comply with the law's requirements. In addition to the retrofitting, a formal committee comprising a voluntary working group was formed.

Corporate social responsibility comes in a variety of shapes and sizes. A modest gift to a local food bank may have a big influence on social change, even for the tiniest businesses. The following are some of the most popular CSR examples:

- Carbon footprint reduction
- Labor policies that are more favourable
- Fairtrade participation
- Inclusion, diversity, and equity
- Philanthropic giving worldwide
- Volunteering in the community and online
- Environmentally friendly corporate policies
- Investments that are both socially and ecologically aware.

CSR Statutory Obligations In India

Companies that fall under the following categories are required to participate in CSR under the Companies Act of 2013:

Companies with a net worth of at least Rs. 500 crore, a turnover of at least Rs. 1,000 crore, or a net profit of at least Rs. 5 crore are eligible.Among the organizational researchers who have attempted to identify and describe the various forms of CSR from time to time, the "Four-Part Model of Corporate Social Responsibility," proposed by Archie Carroll and later refined by Carroll and Buchholtz, is probably the most established and accepted model of CSR that addresses the forms of CSR.

A company's economic obligations include providing a reasonable return to investors, fair remuneration to employees, and goods at reasonable pricing to customers, among other things. As a result, achieving economic responsibility is the initial layer of accountability as well as the foundation for further accountability. The reality is that all firms must fulfil economic responsibilities in order to thrive in the current era.

Legal implications businesses must follow the law of the nation and play by the rules of the game because of their legal responsibilities. Laws are the codification of society's dos and don'ts. Any firm that wants to be socially responsible must follow the law. There have been several occasions in corporate history where laws have been broken and firms were no longer able to operate. Enron, Union Carbide, Global Trust Bank, and other instructive corporate incidents of societal rejection and boycott include, for example, Enron, Union Carbide, and Global Trust Bank.

Moral Responsibilities pertain to corporate commitments that are correct, equitable, and fair. Following the law, process, and rules and regulations does not always imply that corporate activity is ethical or beneficial. Corporate behaviour that goes beyond the law and contributes to societal well-being is said to be ethical. As a result, companies have an ethical obligation to do what is beneficial to society, even if it goes beyond the rules and regulations. To put it another way, ethical duties are what society expects from companies in addition to their economic and legal obligations.

The Greek term philanthropy literally means "love of one's neighbour." The application of this concept in the business world includes efforts that are, of course, within the corporation's discretion to improve the quality of life of workers, local communities, and, ultimately, society. Corporate Social Responsibility (CSR) has been practised in India for decades.

Strategic CSR

CSR has been a popular topic in recent years as a result of such illustrious instances. Indian CSR is on the rise. The accessibility and efficacy of CSR initiatives are further hampered by a lack of awareness, insufficiently educated employees, coverage, policy, and other factors. A large number of businesses are engaging in these activities on the surface and marketing them in the media. Public relations is an effective strategy for influencing customer perceptions and enhancing a company's image. Corporations that actively promote their social responsibility efforts frequently use the media to highlight their work. Publicizing business donations, staff volunteer programs, and other CSR activities is a strong branding strategy that may help you gain exposure in both online and print media. When it comes to working with politicians and government authorities, companies that prioritise corporate social responsibility usually have an easier time. Businesses that show a reckless disdain for social responsibility, on the other hand, frequently find themselves defending themselves against numerous inquiries and probes, which are frequently initiated at the request of public service groups. The more positive public opinion is, the better.The less likely activist organizations are to initiate public campaigns and seek government investigations against a firm with good public opinion that it takes social responsibility seriously. Finally, one of the most significant advantages of fostering social responsibility at work is the good atmosphere you create for your colleagues. Employees and management will be more excited and involved in their tasks if they believe they work for a firm with a real conscience. This may foster a sense of belonging and collaboration, bringing everyone together and resulting in happier, more productive workers. The fundamental problem for organizations that perceive CSR as a way to grow their company is implementation. A viable path forward can be found through smart cooperation.

Organizational and Strategic CSR Perspectives So, what exactly is Strategic Corporate Social Responsibility (SCSR)? Companies may evaluate what actions they have the resources to spend on being socially responsible and choose those that will increase their competitive advantage by taking a strategic approach. Organizations may guarantee that earnings and increasing shareholder value do not eclipse the requirement to behave ethically toward their stakeholders by including CSR into their entire strategy. • Managing stakeholder relationships (particularly those with opposing values).Strategic CSR provides firms with solutions for balancing the creation of economic value with the creation of societal value; recognising and responding to threats and opportunities that their stakeholders face; and evaluating the organization's capacity for charitable endeavours and sustainable business methods.

CSR in business is the driving force behind all you do. Profit-seeking businesses also contribute to some areas of societal development, but clearly not all. It is unrealistic to expect every corporation to be active in every facet of social development. The expenses of implementing CSR will be higher, but the benefits will almost certainly surpass the expenditures. The terrible events of September 11th have given global issues a new dimension. The fall of Enron and WorldCom, as well as its auditor, Arthur Andersen, as a result of questionable accounting methods, has increased scrutiny of huge corporations and their auditors.

Companies are becoming increasingly aware of the need to project a socially conscious image. When it comes to picking a brand or firm, consumers, workers, and stakeholders value CSR, and they hold corporations accountable for affecting social change via their principles, policies, and profits.

Passion Lilie's creator and chief designer, Katie Schmidt, stated, *"What the public thinks about your company is important to its success."* By cultivating a good image that you believe in, you may establish a reputation for your firm as being socially conscious.

To stand out from the crowd, your business must demonstrate to the public that it is a force for good. Advocating for and raising awareness for socially significant topics is a great approach for your company to stay top-of-mind and boost brand value. According to the Kantar Purpose 2020 study, there is a direct link between perceived positive effect and increased brand value. Over the course of 12 years, companies having a high positive effect grew their brand value by 175 percent, whereas firms with a low positive impact grew by just 70 percent. Schmidt also stated that sustainable development might be beneficial to a company's bottom line. Reduced manufacturing costs can be achieved by using less packaging and less energy, for example.

If you demonstrate a well-developed CSR program and efforts, your firm will become more desirable to existing and potential investors. Investors are becoming more important stakeholders in corporate social responsibility, according to CECP's authoritative 2021 Giving in Numbers report. Almost 80% of the firms polled said they were willing to share data and examine their viewpoints on sustainability. When it comes to social responsibility, investors, like customers, are holding firms accountable. At the same time, a firm that takes CSR seriously sends a message to both investors and partners that it cares about both long-term and short-term success.

CSR's Rewarding Effects

- Innovation By applying the *"lens of sustainability,"* as McDonald put it, Unilever was able to develop new goods such as a water-saving hair conditioner. The company's research and development efforts may not have resulted in such a product if it hadn't been for sustainability.
- Cost-cutting One of the simplest ways for a corporation to become involved in sustainability is to use it as a cost-cutting

tool. General Mills, for example, has set a goal of reducing energy consumption by 20% by 2015.

- Brand differentiation (for example, Timberland), for example, was able to develop their voice and implement their principles into their business strategy.
- Customer participation What good is corporate social responsibility if no one knows about it? Wal-Mart has positioned itself as a leader in environmental measures in recent years. This is an underutilised instrument for company-to-company communication.
- Motivating employeesSara Lee established a cross-functional, worldwide Sustainability Working Team to assist in the development of a sustainability strategy. The Solo Cup Company launched the Sustainability Action Network to engage workers in community service centred on the company's CSR initiatives at a more grassroots level.
- Keeping social responsibility at the forefront of one's thoughts helps firms act ethically and examine their company's social and environmental consequences.
- Giving employees the option to participate in a company's socially responsible initiatives can benefit employees by teaching them new skills that they can apply in the workplace. By engaging in activities outside of their normal job obligations, employees can contribute to projects and issues that they are passionate about or learn something completely new that will assist in improving their own views. Organizations stimulate growth and development by sponsoring these activities. Organizations enhance employee growth and support by sponsoring these activities.
- Increased productivity and quality; improved capacity to recruit and retain employees; reduced regulatory scrutiny; improved access to financing; diversification of the workforce; product safety and liability reduction; contributions to charity; employee volunteer programs; corporate engagement in community education, employment, and homelessness initiatives; product

safety and quality; social advantages: as increased use of renewable resources; integration of environmental management tools into company planning, including life-cycle assessment and costing; assessment and costing, environmental management standards, and eco-labeling.

- It may help existing and prospective clients strengthen links, form alliances, and develop solid business partnerships. As a result, it is possible to achieve public-value results that would not have been possible otherwise.
- Differentiation of Brands CSR can aid in the development of client loyalty based on shared ethical ideals. Some businesses use their commitment to CSR as a major selling point. Some businesses utilise CSR approaches as a strategic tool to acquire public support for their worldwide presence, allowing them to maintain a competitive edge by exploiting their social contributions as another type of advertising. For example, when Dettol developed its cause-related marketing strategy, in which a shilling is contributed to charity for every product purchased, Dettol goods gained appeal in the marketplace, separating themselves from other antibacterial products.

Challenges Of CSR

Long before the term became widespread, companies like Tata and Birla in India have been practising Corporate Social Responsibility (CSR) for decades. Despite having such illustrious precedents, CSR in India is still in its early stages. CSR programs' reach and efficacy are further hampered by a lack of awareness, insufficiently educated people, coverage, policy, and other factors. A large number of firms are engaging in these actions on the surface and promoting and highlighting them in the media. This study paper investigates and evaluates the concerns and obstacles that CSR operations in India confront. Corporate social responsibility has been firmly entrenched in the global business agenda. However, numerous obstacles must be overcome in order to transition from theory to practice. Corporate social responsibility has been firmly entrenched in the global business agenda. However, several difficulties must be overcome in order to get from theory to action. The need for more accurate measures of progress in the field of CSR, as well as the distribution of CSR plans, is a major problem for businesses. Transparency and discussion may help a company look more trustworthy while also raising the standards of other businesses. The following are some of the beneficial consequences that can occur when corporations implement a social responsibility policy:The requirements include spending at least 2% of profits on CSR and establishing a dedicated committee on their board to oversee execution. As a result of this law, India is the only country in the world with a CSR law. In order to comply with the rules of the Enterprises Act, 2013, about 8,500 Indian companies would be obliged to execute CSR initiatives under this new legislation. Many businesses will be taking these steps for the first time. According to estimates, corporate social responsibility commitments might total up to Rs. 20,000 crore every year. CSR has been practised by Indian businesses for decades. Many major corporations, such as Tata, Wipro, and Maruti, have successfully implemented their programs. However, the vast majority of them are still useless. Lack of awareness of the industry and challenges, target recipients, insufficiently trained people, coverage, and other factors all contribute to CSR's ineffectiveness. Some businesses engage in these actions ostensibly for the purpose of promoting them in the media.Major CSR projects are undertaken by Indian corporations. CSR has always been viewed as a charity activity in India. As a result, documentation on particular operations linked to this notion is scarce. However, it was apparent that much of this had a national flavour to it, whether it was endowing institutions or actively engaging in India's liberation fight, and it was encompassed in the concept of trusteeship.The strength of customer pressure knows no bounds. Consumer concerns are taken into account by even major conventional enterprises. For example, Lego has set a goal of using only renewable energy to power its manufacturing facilities.The Danish corporation was able to achieve this target even sooner than expected because of the installation of an offshore wind farm. Wind farm Lego kits are currently available. One step companies are taking to boost this sort of consumer reaction is by working to be a *"millennial-friendly"* firm to create trust with community members. An organization that is prepared to produce or support socially responsible projects demonstrates to customers that they have the value alignment that their target audience seeks, whether it be through waste reduction, charitable giving, or encouraging opportunities in their community.

As several commentators have noted, CSR in India is still mostly philanthropic, but it has shifted from institutional construction (educational, scientific, and cultural) to community development through various initiatives. Furthermore, as global influences and communities become more active and demanding, there appears to be a discernible trend that, while CSR remains largely limited to community development, it is becoming more strategic in nature (i.e., becoming linked to business) than philanthropic, and a large number of companies are reporting their activities in this space on their official websites, annual reports, sustainability reports, and even publishing books.

If a company does not explore waste reduction, clean water efforts, or other environmentally friendly solutions, it will be missing out on a significant market of customers who want to buy from companies that are socially responsible and sustainable, as well as companies that share their values. This is a setback.

When it comes to developing a socially responsible company strategy, there are a few things to avoid. It is possible to become a socially responsible business with a few restrictions. Avoid volunteering for charitable causes that are unrelated to your primary business or that in any way contradict your company's ethical standards. Instead of giving money to a completely unrelated group, find a nonprofit that your firm believes in or invest in a project in your neighbourhood. Don't use CSR opportunities only to promote your company. According to Schmidt, running a corporate responsibility campaign as a fast marketing strategy might backfire if your company doesn't follow through. Rather than attempting a one-time stunt, gradually implement socially acceptable corporate practises. According to Schmidt, employees and customers respond favourably to businesses that prioritise long-term social responsibility. Don't wait for the rest of the industry to catch up to you. Don't delay if you're thinking of sustainable actions that aren't yet legally obligatory. You may set the benchmark for your industry and enhance your process by embracing socially responsible rules early on. Taking part in CSR projects benefits everyone involved. Your actions will not only appeal to socially conscious customers and staff, but they will also have a real world impact.

Global Businesses That Are Serious About CSR

Adidas is fighting plastic pollution by collaborating with Parley to transform garbage into high-performance gear. They've also staged Run For The Oceans events to raise cash since 2018. They're also collaborating with Greenpeace on the DETOX Campaign, which aims to remove hazardous chemicals from global supply chains. This entailed collaborating with other brands in order to meet the campaign's objectives. Starbucks is a supporter of Ethos Water, a global effort that aspires to provide clean water to 1 billion people. The Ethos Water Fund is run by the Starbucks Foundation, and proceeds from the sale of Ethos Water bottles go to support the program. For more than two decades, the Starbucks Foundation has supported local communities in both the United States and throughout the world. For more than two decades, the Starbucks Foundation has been investing in local communities in the United States and across the world. This includes a major focus on groups that assist people in overcoming hurdles to employment and training. Tamana, Grow Trees, KK Academy, and the World Monument Fund are among the organizations with whom IndiGoReach has collaborated. Children, education, female empowerment, the environment, and heritage are all important aspects of their social responsibilities. To date, their collaborations have assisted in the empowerment of over 64,000 women, the education of over 47,000 children, and the planting of over 40,000 trees. IKEA's commitment to social responsibility begins with the materials they use in their goods, which include organic cotton, wool, and wood. By 2030, they intend to use exclusively recycled or renewable plastic. They help more households transcend poverty by establishing a sustainable income through the IKEA Foundation. Climate action, renewable energy, agricultural livelihoods, employment and entrepreneurship, and disaster response are among the programs they support. They collaborate with NGOs and other partners to implement these initiatives. Bosch is committed to investing in programs that assist communities across the world to solve difficulties. To accomplish this, they collaborate with a number of organizations, including the New Sunshine Charity Foundation. Since 2018, Apple has been a Laureate partner with the Malala Fund to help educate and empower girls. Since 2014, they've been members of the ConnectED project, which sponsors teaching and learning solutions in schools across the United States. Coca-Cola distributes at least 1% of its yearly operating profits to charitable organizations and causes. They've been assisting Arwa's "Price of Water" initiative in providing safe drinking water to refugees in the Middle East since 2014. BMW collaborates with groups to achieve their CSR objectives of encouraging diversity, motivating the next generation of engineers, supporting social mobility and inclusion, and educating people about road safety. They also urge their staff to contribute to causes and organizations that they care about. Dell aims to utilise its technology and experience to help the world change for the better. In 2019, their employees volunteered 5 million hours to local charities. This was mostly a skills-based situation. Their technology has been used to improve the Indian government's preventative healthcare system, give speedier treatments for critically ill children, and assist in educating more children throughout the world. Microsoft provides CSR programs that focus on boosting skills and employability as well as environmental sustainability. Through Microsoft Philanthropies, they work with NGOs, organizations, and schools to advance computer science education and create greater impact through technology. They also support groups that work to enhance Washington residents' quality of life. Employee giving is a key element of Microsoft's corporate culture; therefore, workers also support initiatives in their local areas. They provide their time and skills to organizations in addition to donating money. Microsoft matches employee contributions both financially and in terms of time.

If you're seeking CSR ideas for your company, here are some examples of large-scale CSR initiatives.

LEGO has invested millions of dollars in addressing climate change and waste reduction.Reduced packaging, sustainable materials, and investments in alternative energy are among LEGO's ecologically aware endeavours. To promote physical and mental health as well as educational possibilities, TOMS distributes one-third of its net income to organizations. During the epidemic, all charity donations were routed to the TOMS COVID-19 Global Giving Fund. The Johnson & Johnson brand invests in alternative energy sources to reduce its environmental impact. Johnson & Johnson also strives to provide communities with clean, safe water on a global scale. To diversify its staff, the multinational coffee company has adopted a socially responsible recruiting procedure. It is focusing its efforts on hiring more veterans, young people just starting out in their careers, and refugees. By investing in renewable energy sources and environmentally friendly offices, Google has proved its dedication to the environment. Sundar Pichai, the company's CEO, is well known for taking a position on social concerns. Pfizer's commitment to corporate responsibility is evident in its healthcare activities, which include raising awareness about non-infectious illnesses and providing affordable health care to women and children in developing countries. These businesses are taking significant steps to better their communities and the globe in general. These 10 projects set the standard for this year's most creative enterprises in the field of corporate social responsibility, from sustainably made shoes to mitigating 75 years of carbon waste.

Most innovative Companies in the field of corporate social responsibility in 2021 are:

Microsoft:

Setting extremely lofty long-term carbon-neutrality targets. Not only is Microsoft vowing to become carbon neutral by 2030, but also to erase all of the carbon the firm has ever released since its creation in 1975 by 2050, going above and beyond most conventional corporate climate promises.It plans to do so by establishing a climate-related innovation fund, growing its internal carbon charge, and assisting suppliers and customers in reducing their carbon footprints. And, in order to reach zero waste by 2030, it has made the daring promise of diverting at least 90% of its landfill trash and making all Surface devices totally recyclable.

Grove Collaborative:

For pledging to eliminate all plastic from its products. It plans to do so by establishing a climate-related innovation fund, growing its internal carbon charge, and assisting suppliers and customers in reducing their carbon footprints. And, in order to reach zero waste by 2030, it has made the daring promise of diverting at least 90% of its landfill trash and making all Surface devices totally recyclable.This natural goods shop aspires to be completely plastic-free by 2025. In 2020, it took a step toward that aim by developing a 100% plastic-free range of household cleaning goods that instead use glass and aluminium containers. It also introduced Peach, a new personal care line of waterless, plastic-free, plant-based products that the company hopes will save 70,000 pounds of plastic in less than a year of sales.

Capital One

Over the course of the summer, the company's Capital One Coders summer program grew by 400 percent, transitioning to a virtual classroom format to engage predominantly low-to-moderate-income children in technology through problem-solving methodologies. To teach about AI, it added an app creator and a bot camp to its extended curriculum. They also provided much-needed digital connectivity to 2,500 households at a time when many youngsters without access to Wi-Fi have struggled to attend virtual classes.

Logitech

That is unrivalled in the industry for its clarity on carbon emissions.The consumer electronics design firm has committed to "complete carbon transparency," pledging to mark all goods with a carbon footprint figure. By 2025, it hopes to have those numbers—along with universally accessible symbols—printed throughout its entire portfolio, allowing customers to make educated decisions and hold the company responsible.

Clio

In collaboration with the American Bar Association, this Canadian legal cloud software business launched a pro-bono platform to link attorneys with those in need of legal assistance for concerns related to the epidemic, such as housing, unemployment benefits, and domestic abuse. Clio's main objective is to remove financial obstacles to legal representation, and this invention is part of that mission.

Verizon

As the pandemic spread, Verizon Innovative Learning ramped up its efforts to provide under-resourced schoolchildren with their own built-in technology devices and free data plans, allowing them to comfortably engage in distance learning and overcome the "digital divide" that has left so many low-income children reliant on Wi-Fi from nearby buildings. They've also blended sophisticated technology into learning: in Miami, enrolled students functioned as IT troubleshooters for school systems transitioning to virtual learning, while others in Cleveland 3D-printed personal protective equipment for important employees.

Bitwise Industries

As the epidemic spread, this tech ecosystem pledged to combine its specialised knowledge to create digital initiatives that would help underprivileged people gain access to the necessities they so sorely needed. Its software engineers created an app to manage grocery orders and track food delivery, resulting in 200,000 meals being delivered across California's Central Valley. Separately, it launched a network that connected newly jobless individuals with employment and assistance, initially in California with Governor Newsom's support, and later across much of the United States.

CSR is an increasing trend among corporations, and it's also a wonderful method for NGOs to diversify their revenue and reach out to new supporters. Companies that are socially responsible are putting their resources to good use in their communities (both local and global). Many NGOs aren't realising the benefits of CSR collaborations, owing to a lack of knowledge about how to get started. Even if your business is tiny, you may still benefit from bringing in CSR partners and using their cash, resources, and support to promote your cause.

By caring about problems like Earth Day, raising awareness, and encouraging social change, corporate social responsibility helps build customer trust. Thousands of firms are contributing, but the activities of huge multinational corporations have far-reaching consequences that can affect global concerns such as hunger and health, as well as global warming and climate change.

India's CSR Development

At the initial stage Charity and philanthropy were the primary motivations for CSR in the early stages. Wealthy merchants shared a portion of their riches with the wider society during the pre-industrialization period, which lasted until 1850, by erecting temples for religious purposes. Industrial dynasties such as Tata, Godrej, Bajaj, Modi, Birla, and Singhania were highly influenced by economic and social issues in the nineteenth century. However, it has been recognised that their efforts toward social and industrial progress were affected by caste groupings and political interests in addition to unselfish and religious objectives. During the second phase of the independence struggle, there was a greater emphasis on Indian industrialists' demonstrating their commitment to the advancement of society. This was the time when Mahatma Gandhi created the concept of *"trusteeship,"* which required business executives to manage their riches in order to help the common man. The Final Stage The third phase of CSR (1960–80) was linked to the *"mixed economy"* feature, the creation of public sector undertakings (PSUs), and labour and environmental legislation. The Final Stage Indian corporations began abandoning their conventional CSR participation in the fourth phase (1980–2013) and integrating it into a long-term business plan. CSR in India is undergoing a transformation. The Corporate Social Responsibility (CSR) law went into force on April 1, 2014, and it's been a little over a year since then. The entire landscape of CSR in India has undergone a drastic turn in such a short time. Companies that are qualified under section 135 of the Companies Act 2013 have embraced the law and launched a slew of CSR initiatives across the board, as stated in Schedule VII of the Act.

CSR encompasses not only the development activities that a company performs but also the processes that a corporation uses to make responsible investments and provide transparency to diverse stakeholders, among other things. Recognizing the value of socially responsible business practises, they have implemented them. CSR's main goal is to optimise a company's total influence on society and stakeholders while also addressing the environment and long-term viability. Paternalistic philanthropy has a long history in India. CSR encompasses not only the development activities that a company performs but also the techniques that a firm is responsible for. Despite its newfound popularity, the method has been used since ancient times, although unofficially. Philosophers from India, such as Kautilya, and philosophers from the pre-Christian era in the West, advocated and encouraged ethical ideals in business.Several ancient texts mention the principle of assisting the poor and disadvantaged. Philanthropy, religion, and charity were the primary drivers of CSR prior to the industrial revolution. Charity and other social issues were important to industrial households in the nineteenth century. However, the payments, whether monetary or non-monetary, were occasional acts of charity or philanthropy made from personal funds that did not belong to the shareholders and did not form part of the business. The industrial families also built temples, schools, higher education institutions, and other public facilities during this time. In the early 1970s, the term "corporate social responsibility" became popular. The last ten years of the twentieth century saw a change in emphasis away from charity and conventional philanthropy and toward more direct commercial participation in mainstream development and concern for underprivileged sections of society. There is a growing recognition in India that business cannot flourish in isolation and that social change is required for long-term success. In India, where there is a huge divide between parts of the population in terms of income and standards, as well as socio-economic position, an ideal CSR approach incorporates both ethical and philosophical components.CSR has expanded fast in India over the last decade, with some corporations concentrating on strategic CSR activities to help improve the country. Companies in India gradually began to focus on need-based programs that coincided with national goals, including public health, education, livelihoods, water conservation, and natural resource management. In the last 10 years, there have been extensive national discussions about the business sector's possible role and duty in addressing social challenges.In its emphasis on getting businesses to join in solving social and developmental challenges as part of their social responsibility and business operations, The Department of Public Enterprises released standards for spending on CSR initiatives for central public sector enterprises, setting an example for the private sector.

CSR Activities of India's Top Companies

In 2021, the Sustainable Development Goals (SDGs) will be included in the responsible business actions of 80% of the top 100 firms for sustainability and CSR. CSR had an especially bad year in the year 2021. In comparison to the previous year, CSR expenditure in the country declined by 64% in FY 2020–21. CSR spending in the past financial year amounted to Rs. 8,828.11 crore, according to official statistics given to the federal legislative body, a significant decrease from Rs. 24,688.66 crore in FY 2019–20 and Rs. 20,150.27

crore in FY 2018–19.Godrej Consumer Goods has topped the CSR rating list for the first time in 2021, followed by Infosys and Wipro, which have been continuous star performers. In addition, two Tata enterprises rank among the top ten. In FY 2021, IT was the best-performing industry in terms of CSR. Godrej Consumer Products Limited is a company that manufactures consumer goods. In the fiscal year 2020–21, Godrej Consumer Products Ltd. (GCPL) spent Rs. 34.08 crore on CSR projects. Over 2.77 lakh people from the most vulnerable groups were addressed by the company's CSR programs. GCPL redirected 63% of their CSR funding to start medium-to long-term livelihood recovery programs for over 9000 nano entrepreneurs during the previous fiscal year. The majority of its CSR projects have been carried out through the Infosys Foundation, which was founded in 1996, long before the nation's CSR mandate was lifted. The firm spent Rs. 325.32 crores on CSR projects in FY 2020–21. Wipro's CSR initiatives are carried out through a variety of channels, the most prominent of which being the Wipro Foundation. In the previous financial year, the firm spent Rs. 251 crores on CSR. Wipro has sponsored over 1,561 initiatives spanning humanitarian relief, integrated healthcare, and livelihood regeneration in the previous 12 months, with a total impact of over 10 million people as a result of its COVID-19 response. As a result, over 10.2 million people have received food, dry rations, and personal hygiene kits. As a result, 330 million meals have been distributed, over 8.2 million people have had their livelihoods restored, and more than 500 non-profits involved in humanitarian and healthcare aid have been supported. Through mohalla lessons, distribution of worksheets, books, and other materials, the company's education efforts were helpful in reaching over 1.1 lakh pupils throughout 14 states. Tata Chemicals has been one of the most prominent sustainability champions in recent years. The organization has undertaken a number of environmental initiatives and projects, as well as working with local communities to create a sustainable and environmentally friendly environment. In FY21, the company spent Rs. 21 crore on CSR initiatives. In the previous financial year, the firm helped 6,878 farmers with capacity building, field demonstrations, and livestock management through digital and physical contacts. It also supported Okhai's rural women artisans, transforming the region into a bazaar with 25,190 participants. Through mohalla lessons, distribution of worksheets, books, and other materials, the company's education efforts were helpful in reaching over 1.1 lakh pupils throughout 14 states. It also supported Okhai's rural women artisans, transforming the region into a marketplace that connects 25,190 craftsmen from throughout India with buyers. At Mithapur, the corporation has planted 1.15 lakh mangroves across several areas as part of its greening effort, which also includes the protection of native plant species. The concept that an organization must serve a greater societal purpose while keeping national interests in mind drives ITC's sustainability activities. The company's mission to concurrently develop economic, social, and environmental capital, known as the Triple Bottom Line, has choreographed a symphony of attempts to solve some of the most difficult societal concerns, such as pervasive poverty and environmental degradation. The company's social forestry initiative greened 30,439 acres of land in the previous fiscal year. Through its education initiative, the corporation was able to reach 0.33 million youngsters. During the year, it supplied skills to 12,470 young people through vocational training programs. In 28 areas, it helped fund the building of 640 individual family toilets. Jubilant Life Sciences Limited was ranked in the top ten corporations for CSR this year, up from 23rd the previous year. The Jubilant Bhartia Foundation is in charge of the majority of Jubilant Life Sciences' CSR projects. Through several social development programs in the realms of health, education, livelihood, and social entrepreneurship, the company's CSR actions are reaching out to nearly 6.5 million people in 240 communities. Grasim Industries Limited has increased its CSR spending by nearly 45 percent since the previous fiscal year.In FY 2020–21, it spent Rs. 84.66 crores, up from Rs. 47.14 crores in FY20. The Economic Times and Futurescape Responsible Business Rankings 2020 named it 9th among India's Top Companies for Sustainability and CSR. This year, it has risen to 7th place on the list. Grasim's social outreach network spans 15 places in India, encompassing seven states. Through its CSR initiatives, the firm was able to affect the lives of nearly 31.6 lakh individuals in FY21. Since the previous fiscal year, Grasim Industries Limited has increased its CSR spending by nearly 45 percent.In FY 2020–21, it spent Rs. 84.66 crores, up from Rs. 47.14 crores in FY20. The Economic Times and Futurescape Responsible Business Rankings 2020 named it 9th among India's Top Companies for Sustainability and CSR. This year, it has risen to 7th place on the list. Grasim's social outreach network spans 15 places in India, encompassing seven states. Through its CSR initiatives, the firm was able to affect the lives of nearly 31.6 lakh individuals in FY21. Vedanta Limited is involved in a variety of CSR efforts, including water, energy, and carbon management. Across our core impact areas of education, health, sustainable livelihoods, women's empowerment, sports and culture, environment, and community development, Vedanta spent approximately Rs. 331 crore on social development programs in FY2021.

Tata Power has climbed to number 10 in the CSR rankings, up from 57th the previous year. In 2020-21, the electric utility firm spent Rs. 3.45 crore on CSR. Financial inclusion, education, health and sanitation, water, livelihoods and skill building are the five main areas of its CSR projects. JSW Steel Limited believes that superior goods, sustained growth, and CSR activities create value for all of its stakeholders. In the fiscal year 2020–21, the firm spent Rs. 78.32 crores on CSR, with an extra Rs. 86.49 crores put into the unspent CSR account. UPL is a global agricultural goods and solutions company. In India, the corporation paid Rs. 100 crore for CSR, with Rs. 75 crore going to the PM CARES Fund to combat the epidemic. The CSR team undertook multiple activities around the country in 2020–21 to satisfy the development requirements of various communities. As part of Project Pace in Pratapgarh and Sultanpur, UPL is assisting the TYCIA Foundation in delivering better education. UPL will finance the education of 100 kids as part of this effort, which will also include the creation of basic infrastructure. The business has built 120 solar lights in Rajasthan's Barmer and 95 solar lights in Madhya Pradesh's Singhbara and Morena. During the fiscal years 2020–21, Mahindra & Mahindra Ltd. invested Rs. 92.78 crore in different CSR initiatives across India. This figure excludes the company's Rs. 20 crore commitment to the PM CARES Fund in FY 2020. M & M Ltd. is a company based in the United Kingdom. Dr. Reddy's Laboratories is a Hyderabad-based international pharmaceutical firm. This year, it spent more on corporate social responsibility than was required. The pharma business spent Rs. 36.08 crores on CSR in FY2021, instead of the mandated Rs. 34.1 crores. During the three years prior to the current financial year, Tech Mahindra spent more than 2% of its average net income on CSR. The corporation made a major contribution to COVID-19 relief efforts this year. A total of Rs. 105 crore was spent on corporate social responsibility programs.The TMF team altered its focus as soon as the COVID-19 epidemic broke out, to provide help to those who were the worst impacted—daily wagers, migrant workers, farmers, people with disabilities, and the transgender community. The Foundation supplied over 6 lakh ration packages, 3.20 lakh prepared meals, PPE kits, masks, and medical equipment to hospitals through systematic and effective action. Over the course of the year, relief activities of Rs. 14.82 crores were carried out, with work continuing into the current financial year. Over 20 million individuals have benefited from these initiatives to date. In addition to the government's efforts to combat COVID-19, Hindustan Unilever was one of the first companies to pledge Rs. 100 crores to societal activity. In FY2021, the corporation spent Rs. 165.08 crores on corporate social responsibility. In partnership with the government and various NGOs, HUL donated over 2 crore soaps and sanitisers, bottles of toilet and surface cleaners, Horlicks packs, and other products to frontline medical professionals, police officers, sanitation workers, and vulnerable citizens of the country in a partnership with the government and various NGOs during the pandemic. Ambuja

Cement is a significant participant in the Indian cement market and is known for its custom-made product line that is appropriate for a variety of climatic situations in India. In FY2021, Rs. 53.97 crores were spent on CSR initiatives, significantly more than the mandated amount. Toyota Kirloskar Motor (TKM) is a joint venture between Toyota Motor Corporation Japan and Kirloskar Systems Limited that was founded in India in 1997. Toyota's position in the global automotive environment serves as motivation for TKM. By promoting active local engagement, the firm thinks it can create localised solutions that are sustainable. In this context, the CSR team has designed and constructed a sustainable community development model, in which basic community interventions at the local level are made.In this context, the CSR team has designed and constructed a long-term community development model in which basic community interventions are refined over time into more strategic and comprehensive collaborations. Long before the Companies Act of 2013 compelled CSR, L & T was providing health and educational services to the needy in the communities surrounding its campuses. L & T's CSR programs are well-established now, concentrating on sectors that match with global and national development objectives, such as water and sanitation, health, education, and skill development. In FY 2020-21, total CSR spending was Rs. 150.06 crores, or 2.062 percent of earnings after tax, which is higher than the minimum 2%.L & T's CSR has been on the frontlines in a variety of ways, including establishing ICUs for treating COVID-19 patients, equipping government hospitals with ventilators, providing Personal Protective Equipment (PPE) kits, gloves, and masks to health workers, and making basic provisions such as food available to those in need. The majority of the CSR program employees accepted responsibility for educating communities in the project areas about preventative and safety measures, and they were accessible for counselling and referrals. NTPC Limited, India's largest power company, is a statutory Indian business. In the fiscal year 2020–21, it spent Rs. 418.87 crore on CSR projects, exceeding the mandated 2 percent amount of Rs.

278.57 crore and achieving a CSR expenditure of 3.04 percent.The corporation donated Rs. 250 crores to the PM CARES Fund to aid the government's fight against COVID-19. NTPC earned the FICCI Jury Commendation Certificate under the Category "Women Empowerment" for its flagship CSR project "Girl Empowerment Mission" at the CII-ITC Sustainability Award-2020 for "Corporate Social Responsibility" (GEM). Hindustan Zinc is the world's sixth largest silver producer and India's sole integrated silver, lead, and zinc producer. HZL is a subsidiary of Vedanta Limited, which owns 64.9 percent of the firm, while the Indian government holds 29.5 percent. In FY2021, HZL spent Rs. 214 crores on CSR. The "Integrated Health and Wellbeing Council" awarded Hindustan Zinc the CSR Health Effect Award in 2021 as a symbol of gratitude for its extraordinary reaction and on-the-ground activities with a strong focus on life, livelihood, and mitigating the impact of the COVID-19 epidemic.

Companies that are socially responsible use their power and resources for more than just gratifying their shareholders and expanding their profits. They use a business strategy that emphasises social impact and rewards their local and global communities for their achievements. This isn't to suggest that profit is unimportant to socially conscious businesses (probably not the most sustainable step for for-profit companies).No, businesses are simply accepting their duty to improve the well-being of the communities from which they profit and are weaving that responsibility into the fabric of their operations. Companies are increasingly incorporating corporate social responsibility (CSR) programs into their operations and associating themselves with social movements that are gaining traction. CSR strategies vary with each company, but they often include charitable fundraising, working conditions, social benefits such as health care, volunteerism, and environmental stewardship. And other businesses go beyond a program to make social responsibility a part of their DNA. While it's unknown if firms like JP Morgan and Amazon will act to meet their pledges to social justice and sustainability, the trend is clear: companies recognise that customers value the good of society over the good of the company's shareholders, and they're responding accordingly.

Millennials want more corporate social responsibility. Socially responsible businesses are much more essential to millennials and Generation Z. They think that businesses should invest in improving society and seek out solutions that would help them do so. Companies should communicate how they are attempting to have a beneficial influence on the globe so that the general public may witness their pro-social efforts. It's critical to understand how to sell to millennials since your efforts will influence the decisions they make as customers. Millennials also like to participate in activities such as volunteer work and philanthropy. As more businesses see the influence of their socially and environmentally conscious initiatives on consumer perception, the more likely it is that they will follow suit. As more organizations see the influence of their socially and ecologically conscious activities on customer perception, the more likely they are to launch their own projects. As Millennials and Gen Z become the economy's driving force, appreciation for socially responsible corporate practises continues to grow. As a result of these two generations' purchasing perspectives, consumer attention has turned to social responsibility, particularly when it comes to the environment. According to a Nielsen survey conducted in 2018, 85 percent of Millennials and 80 percent of Gen Z regard the environment as the most important factor in deciding which companies to connect with.

CSR is a means for businesses to give back to the community and assist groups that share their values. Matching gift schemes, gifts of dollars or products, and volunteer grant programs are all examples of this. In addition to the altruistic aspects, a corporate social responsibility program may help firms differentiate themselves from their competition. Enhanced brand image, higher media coverage, improved consumer loyalty, and additional investment prospects are just a few of the advantages. Many well-known companies have embraced CSR and joined with a variety of charitable organizations to effect change. With their CSR activities, many socially responsible businesses have a direct influence on society. Consumers believe that by purchasing a product or service from a socially responsible firm, they are helping to make the world a better place. The more socially responsible a firm is, the more its community and customers support it.According to studies, consumers are increasingly prepared to spend extra when they know their purchases will have a positive impact. Consumer decision-making has been demonstrated to be influenced by environmental friendliness alone, with a rising percentage of customers throughout the world expressing interest in and readiness to pay for ecologically friendly items. Customers are active participants in the world-saving quest to prevent climate change, and they're eager to support the businesses that are fighting with them. The effect isn't entirely external. Employees are asking more and more if their job has a beneficial social impact. Employees are increasingly seeking social fulfilment from their hours spent on the job at a time when the barrier between work and personal life is becoming increasingly blurred.

2021 World Top Brands' CSR Aspirations

Rank 1. Johnson & Johnson, Inc.

Rank 2. Google

Rank 3. Coca-Cola

Rank 4. Ford Motors

Rank 5. Netflix

Rank 6. Spotify

Rank 7. Pfizer

Rank 8. Wells Fargo

Rank 9. Toms

Rank 10. Bosch

Rank 11. General Electric

Rank 12. Starbucks

Rank 13. The Walt Disney

Rank 14. Lego

Coca-Cola is putting a lot of emphasis on sustainability as a brand. Climate, packaging, and agriculture, as well as water stewardship and product quality, are all important considerations. Their mission is to create *"a world without waste,"* with the goal of collecting and recycling every bottle, making all packaging 100% recyclable, and returning all water used in the production of their beverages to the environment to maintain water security. They intend to minimize their carbon impact by 25% by 2030. Ford has big aspirations for corporate social responsibility. They say they want to *"build a better society where everyone is free to move and follow their goals."* They have boosted their investment in electrification to $22 billion (up from $11 billion) and aim to achieve carbon-neutral vehicles by 2050. Johnson & Johnson, a giant in the pharmaceutical industry, is an excellent example of CSR in action. They've been working to reduce their environmental impact for the past three decades. Their initiatives range from wind energy harvesting to providing clean water to people all around the world. The corporation was able to reduce pollution while also offering a sustainable and cost-effective alternative to electricity after purchasing a privately held energy supplier in the Texas Panhandle. The company is still on the lookout for renewable energy options, with the goal of obtaining 100% of its energy from renewable sources. The corporation is still exploring renewable energy sources to cover its whole energy needs by 2025. Sundar Pichai, Google's outspoken CEO, is trusted not only for his environmentally friendly projects, but also for his outspokenness. Google also received the top CSR 2018 score from the Reputation Institute, thanks in part to its data centres consuming 50% less energy than companies across the world. They've also pledged over $1 billion to renewable energy projects and use services like Gmail to help other businesses decrease their environmental impact. When a calamity hits, immediate medical help is critical. Pfizer has a three-pronged approach to help in these situations: product contributions, funding, and access solutions. In the aftermath of Hurricane Matthew and the worldwide refugee crisis in Europe and the Middle East, grants have been given to nations like Haiti. This money is supplied in collaboration with non-governmental organizations (NGOs) in order to reach as many individuals as possible. From a social standpoint, firms like Netflix and Spotify provide advantages to their employees and their families. Netflix provides both birth parents and non-birth parents with 52 weeks of paid parental leave (which includes adopted children). This can be done at any time throughout the first year of a child's life or at any other time that is convenient for them. In comparison, other significant tech businesses had a median of 18 weeks. Spotify has a similar policy, but for a shorter period of paid vacation of 24 weeks. According to the firm, the start of this program resulted in a surge in external employment applications that hasn't subsided. During the COVID-19 epidemic, Pfizer gave $5 million through its Global Medical Grants program to help enhance patient detection, diagnosis, treatment, and management. In addition, funding was made available to clinics, medical centres, and hospitals in order to enhance COVID-19 patient treatment and outcomes. Each year, Wells Fargo donates up to 1.5 percent of its profits to over 14,500 non-profit organizations (NGOs), including food banks and incubators (plant science and renewable energy) to help new businesses get to market faster. The corporation gave $6.25 million to fund a domestic and worldwide response to the COVID-19 epidemic. A total of $1 million will go to the CDC Foundation, $250,000 will go to the International Medical Corps in 30 countries, and $5 million will go to local initiatives to meet community needs. Toms' purpose is to provide a pair of shoes for every pair sold, which has resulted in almost 100 million pairs of shoes being donated to children in need. These earnings have gone toward helping the visually handicapped by giving prescription glasses and medical care, as well as supplying "safe" drinking water and establishing enterprises in poor nations to generate jobs. Bosch established lofty environmental objectives for itself, aiming to lessen its ecological impact through climate action, water conservation, and a circular economy. This commitment appears to have paid off, since 400 of its sites are now climate neutral, paving the way for other multinational corporations. The corporation is currently concentrating on lowering upstream and downstream (product consumption) costs by 15% in 2030. Ecomagination, GE's renewable business strategy, was created more than a decade ago with the goal of doubling down on clean technology and generating $20 billion in sales from green products. As part of its *"Ecomagination Challenge,"* announced last year, GE granted five entrepreneurs $100,000 each to develop their concepts, including an inflatable wind turbine, an intelligent water metre, a cyber-secure network architecture, and short-circuiting and outage technologies, as part of its *"Ecomagination Challenge."* When it came to hiring, Starbucks sought to diversify its workforce and give opportunities to specific cohorts. As part of its socially responsible activities, it has vowed to recruit 25,000 US military veterans and spouses by 2025. The firm accomplished this milestone six years ahead of expectations and currently employs 5,000 veterans and military spouses each year. Starbucks established a mentoring initiative to link black, indigneous, and people of colour (BIPOC) to top executives and engage in partnerships as part of its ongoing efforts to address racial and social fairness. By 2025, the chain hopes to have 30% of BIPOC employees in corporate roles and 40% in retail and production.In their 2020 CSR report, Disney stated that they want to reduce their carbon footprint by committing to zero net greenhouse gas emissions, zero waste, and water conservation. They are aggressively enforcing strong international labour standards to protect their employees' safety and rights. They are also involved in the community and urge their workers to participate as well. When their parks closed due to the COVID-19 outbreak, Disney concentrated their CSR efforts on local communities. They donated $27 million in food and personal protective equipment (PPE) from shuttered parks and production sets, and they urged staff to help virtually.Lego plans to invest $400 million over the next three years, with an emphasis on boosting its sustainability initiatives. As a modern-day superbrand, its key goal is to phase out single-use plastic packaging for its bricks by 2025, with all packaging being sustainable. In collaboration with the Forest Stewardship Council, they will test paper bags in boxes starting in 2021. They're also putting money into more environmentally friendly items that produce no waste and are carbon neutral.

A Checklist for CSR

- Provide a safer working environment and educational resources to employees?
- Would you like to improve your contractual relationships with your employees?
- Is it possible to use more energy-efficient appliances or vehicles?
- Are you sourcing more from local vendors? Is it possible to raise customer service standards?
- Would you want to contribute to more local community projects?
- Do you buy fair-trade items to help workers?
- Is it possible to recycle more waste?
- Make yourself more accessible to customers of varying abilities?

Summing Up

CSR has been the subject of several discussions and studies over the last few years. CSR is a type of self-regulation that represents a company's accountability and commitment to contributing to the well-being of communities and society. CSR aims to enhance communities, the economy, and the environment. Corporate social responsibility is a sort of self-regulation practised by businesses with the goal of social accountability and a positive influence on society. Corporations that actively promote their social responsibility efforts frequently use the media to highlight their work. When it comes to developing a socially responsible company strategy, there are a few things to avoid. One of the most significant advantages of fostering social responsibility at work is the good atmosphere you create for your colleagues. Companies should communicate how they are attempting to have a beneficial influence on the globe so that the general public may witness their pro-social efforts. Socially responsible businesses are much more essential to millennials and Generation Z. As more businesses see the influence of their socially and environmentally conscious initiatives on consumer perception, the more likely it is that they will follow suit. As a result of these two generations' purchasing perspectives, consumer attention has turned to social responsibility, particularly when it comes to the environment.

CHAPTER FIVE

ORGANIZATIONAL OMBUDSMAN

Opportunities For Systemic Change For The Organization

"Play fair, be prepared for others to play dirty, and don't let them drag you into the mud."- Richard Branson

Ombudsman

An organizational Ombudsman is a neutral or impartial dispute resolution practitioner whose primary responsibility is to provide independent, impartial, confidential, and informal assistance to managers and employees, clients, and/or other stakeholders of a corporation, university, or non-governmental organization. Ombudsman (om budz man) is a Swedish term that literally means *"representative."* At its most basic level, an Ombudsman is a person who aids individuals and groups in resolving disagreements or problems. This post is known by a variety of titles and names, including *"Ombudsman," "ombudsperson,"* and *"ombuds."* The classical Ombudsman first arose in Sweden in the early nineteenth century as an independent high-level public official who was appointed by constitutional or legislative provisions to supervise government administrative actions and was answerable to the parliament or legislature. This approach has been imitated and altered in a variety of ways in a variety of nations and environments. Organizational Ombudsmen, classical Ombudsmen, and advocate Ombudsmen are all various sorts of ombudsmen with varied functions, functional tasks, and norms of practice. The main responsibilities of an organizational Ombudsman are to work with individuals and groups within an organization to explore and assist them in determining options for resolving conflicts, problematic issues, or concerns, as well as to bring systemic concerns to the organization's attention for resolution. Some organizational ombuds are hired from inside an organization, accepting this post after demonstrating the above-mentioned qualities and establishing a well-known reputation for integrity, confidentiality, and awareness of organizational procedures across functions in prior roles. When recruiting from the outside, a company would frequently look for someone with a background in dispute resolution and/or who has earned a reputation as an Ombudsman via past organizational experience. Ombudsmen who come from outside the organization, with no prior experience or connections, may be able to offer new viewpoints, and the perception of neutrality may be reinforced. Organizations may also employ the services of an independent Ombudsman.

An organizational Ombudsman is a designated neutral or impartial dispute resolution practitioner whose primary responsibility is to provide independent, impartial, confidential, and informal assistance to managers and employees, clients, and/or other stakeholders of a corporation, university, non-governmental organization, government agency, or other entity. The organizational Ombudsman should ideally have no other job or responsibilities as an independent and unbiased employee. This is to ensure independence and neutrality, as well as to avoid actual or apparent conflicts of interest. An organizational Ombudsman gives opportunities for people with problems, including whistleblowers, who want to bring their complaints forward securely and effectively, using an alternative dispute resolution (ADR) mindset. Additionally, an organizational Ombudsman gives counselling on ethics and other management concerns, facilitates dispute resolution through mediation, and assists in the development of policies. Additionally, an organizational Ombudsman gives coaching on ethics and other management concerns, provides mediation to aid dispute resolution, assists people who feel harassed or discriminated against, and helps permit safe upward feedback. The organizational Ombudsman, in general, aids employees and managers in navigating bureaucracy and dealing with complaints and issues.

Employers who were unaware of the traditional Ombudsman function but recognized the advantage of a senior manager who is a neutral, impartial, confidential, and informal problem-solver and systems change agent have frequently re-invented the role of organizational Ombudsman. Examples first arose in the United States in the 1920s, and they are likely to have appeared in a variety of civilizations. In many businesses, the organizational Ombudsman is viewed as a component of or a link to a complaint system, but the office is designed to operate independently of all normal line and staff management and to report to the CEO or Board of Directors.

Duties Of An Ombudsman

- Listens and comprehends difficulties while keeping an objective when it comes to facts. The Ombudsman does not listen in order to pass judgement or to determine who is correct or incorrect. The Ombudsman listens to comprehend the problem from the individual's point of view. This is a crucial phase in the process of creating resolution possibilities.
- Ombudsman assists in rephrasing difficulties and formulating and evaluating choices for individuals. This assists people in identifying the various parties' interests in the issues and focusing efforts on potential solutions to suit those interests. Individuals are guided or coached on how to interact directly with other parties, including how to use the organization's formal resolution options. An Ombudsman frequently strives to assist people in improving their ability and confidence in

directly expressing their problems.

- Individuals are sent to relevant services for conflict resolution. An Ombudsman may connect people to one or more official organizational resources that may be able to help them resolve their problems.
- Ombudsman assists in bringing concerns to the attention of official resolution mechanisms. When a person is unable or reluctant to express a complaint directly, the Ombudsman can assist by giving the concern a voice and/or raising awareness of the issue among competent decision-makers within the organization.
- Ombudsman facilitates informal conflict settlement. An Ombudsman can assist parties in resolving disputes through various forms of informal mediation.
- Ombudsman identifies new concerns and possibilities for the organization's structural change. The ombuds' unique position allows them to share unedited information that can lead to better understanding and resolution of situations. The Ombudsman is a source of new issue discovery and early warning, as well as systemic reform ideas to enhance existing systems.

Ombudsman' Skills- Roles-Responsibilities

- Active listening, effective communication with a diverse range of people, remaining nonjudgmental, having the courage to speak up and address problems at higher levels within an organization, problem-solving and analytical ability, and conflict resolution skills are among the most important skills of an effective ombudsperson. The acquisition and demonstration of the skill set indicated above is more significant than a specific professional history or academic degree.
- Outstanding ombudspeople from a variety of professional and academic backgrounds, including scientists, human resource experts, mediators, academics, line managers, engineers, attorneys, accountants, and consultants.

- The Ombudsman hears and comprehends concerns while staying objective in his or her assessment of the facts. The Ombudsman does not listen in order to pass judgement or to determine who is correct or incorrect. The Ombudsman listens to comprehend the problem from the individual's point of view. This is a crucial phase in the process of creating resolution possibilities.
- The Ombudsman provides support in reframing situations and establishing and evaluating choices for individuals. This aids people in identifying the interests of various parties involved in the issues and concentrating efforts on them.
- There is no cost, it is independent of the government, and it is non-partisan. Reports on systematic concerns occurring within an agency or with the performance of a government program may be released. Bad practises may be addressed. The State Ombudsman can offer both mediation and investigation. It is impossible to provide a quick response to complicated situations. The complainant has no control over the investigation; the Ombudsman does not explicitly act for the complainant, and they have the authority to refuse to handle a specific case.

Citizens' complaints of abuse of discretionary power, maladministration, or administrative inefficiency are investigated by the Ombudsman, who then takes necessary action. They are given extensive authority for this reason. The complainant is not required to present any proof before the Ombudsman in order to establish his case. The Ombudsman's job and responsibility is to determine whether or not the complaint was legitimate. He's even capable of acting on his own. Ombudsman can provide a remedy to the aggrieved party since, unlike a regular court, his powers are unrestricted. In most cases, the Ombudsman is a judge, a lawyer, or a high-ranking official with impeccable morals, ethics, and probity. Because the Ombudsman is appointed by Parliament, he is not hired by any administrative body or the Executive. Ombudsman is unaffected by political affiliations and is able to think and act rationally. Even Parliament has no say in how he carries out his responsibilities. He submits a report to Parliament detailing citizen reactions to the government. He also offers his own suggestions for removing the sources of complaints. Those reports receive a lot of attention. All of his reports appear in national newspapers as well. In a nutshell, he is the *"watchdog"* or *"public safety valve"* against mal-administration.

Ombudsmen exist for a single purpose: to assist individuals and organizations. They help employees by providing them with someone or a team with whom they can have confidential discussions about bribery, their boss's drug use, sexual harassment, personal conflicts, and other issues. Some employees view HR, compliance officials, and supervisors as business agents whose role it is to safeguard the firm's interests rather than the employees'. They don't know how an investigation will end, and they're frightened the law won't protect them, just like those who are hesitant to report something to the police. This assists people in identifying the various parties' interests in the issues and focusing efforts on potential solutions to suit those interests. The Ombudsman assists or trains people in dealing directly with other parties, including the use of the organization's official resolution options. An Ombudsman frequently strives to assist people in improving their ability and confidence in directly expressing their problems. Individuals are referred to suitable resolution resources by the Ombudsman. An Ombudsman may connect people to one or more official organizational resources that might be able to help them resolve their problems. When conducting investigations, the Ombudsman always takes an objective and unbiased approach while also adhering to procedural fairness. In the course of an inquiry, the Ombudsman obtains confidential information. Some organizational Ombudsmen are hired from inside an organization, accepting this post after demonstrating the above-mentioned qualities and establishing a well-known reputation for honesty, confidentiality, and understanding of organizational procedures across functions in prior roles. When recruiting from the outside, an organization would frequently look for someone with a history of dispute resolution and/or who has earned a reputation as an Ombudsman via previous organizational experience. Ombudsmen who come from outside the organization, with no prior experience or connections, may be able to offer new viewpoints, and the perception of neutrality may be improved. Organizations may also use the services of an independent Ombudsman who is hired on a contract basis.

Making realistic advice concerning serious issues is a priority for the Ombudsman. The Ombudsman will only offer recommendations if he or she believes they would benefit the public. The Ombudsman also evaluates the financial implications of the recommendations for agencies. Ombudsmen provide their services for free, making them available to anyone who cannot afford to pursue their grievances via the courts. They are dedicated to seeking individual remedies as well as systemic reforms in the work of the organizations under their supervision, both individually and collectively, if they find systemic inadequacies. They can usually conduct a single inquiry into many complaints about the same subject, minimising redundancy and unnecessary expense.

Whistleblowing

- What is the definition of a "*whistleblower*"?
- Why do whistleblowers face all kinds of retaliation in the pursuit of the truth?
- What does the whistleblower's abuse cycle look like most of the time?
- How do you blow the whistle without jeopardising your job?
- What may be included in non-disclosure agreement settlements?
- What do whistleblowers have to say about it?
- What can be done to ensure that whistleblowers are protected?

A whistleblower is someone who reveals confidential knowledge or actions that are unlawful, unethical, or incorrect within a business or public institution. The name is claimed to have been invented by Ralph Nader, a prominent American civic activist, in the early 1970s to avoid the negative connotations of words like *"informer"* and *"snitch."* A whistleblower is someone who reports or exposes unlawful, immoral, or unethical action or activity by a person, public company, or private firm. Alternatively, it generates a suspicion of misconduct. Many businesses have their own whistleblower policy, which outlines the kinds of actions that are covered as well as the steps to take if an employee wants to make a protected disclosure. This policy is intended to help and encourage workers to hold the organization and its employees accountable while also promoting strong ethical and moral standards. Whistleblowing occurs when an employee, contractor, or supplier moves outside of the standard management channels to disclose suspected workplace malfeasance, i.e., speaking up in a private way. This can be done through the organization's internal channels (internal whistleblowing) or to an external entity such as a regulator (external whistleblowing). While public disclosure to the media can be seen as whistleblowing, the focus of this study is on formally mandated routes. A worker can report things that aren't right, are unlawful, or if someone at work isn't performing their job, such as:

- Someone's health and safety is at risk
- Environmental damage
- A criminal offence
- The firm isn't following the law
- Covering up wrongdoing

Raising the alarm about problematic practises early enough can help guarantee that issues are discovered before it's too late, preventing tragedies ranging from widespread consumer maltreatment to death. Whistleblowing processes should encourage individuals to report problems through proper channels before they become a severe problem, resulting in unfavourable publicity, regulatory scrutiny, penalties, and/or compensation for the organization. The Whistle Blowers Protection Act, 2011, is an Act passed by the Indian Parliament in 2011 that establishes a mechanism to investigate allegations of public servant corruption and abuse of power, as well as to protect anyone who reports alleged wrongdoing in government bodies, projects, and offices.

- When a whistleblower informs higher-ranking personnel of wrongdoing in a company, disloyalty, inappropriate conduct, indiscipline, insubordination, and disobedience are common topics for internal whistleblowing.
- External whistleblowing occurs when wrongdoings are disclosed to those outside the institution, such as the media, public interest organizations, or law enforcement authorities. Alumni whistleblowing occurs when a former employee of a company acts as a source of information.
- Open whistleblowing occurs when the identity of the whistleblowers is disclosed. Personal whistle blowing occurs when an organization's wrongdoings solely affect one person, and revealing such wrongdoings is referred to as personal whistle blowing.
- When information about wrongdoings or unethical behaviour by government employees becomes public,when a company discloses wrongdoing, it is referred to as corporate whistleblowing.
- Impersonal whistle blowing occurs when the wrongdoing is intended to damage others.

Various whistle-blowers have been threatened, harassed, and even murdered on several occasions. Satyendra Dubey, an engineer, was assassinated in November 2003 after blowing the whistle on a corruption case involving the Golden Quadrilateral project of the National Highways Authority of India. Two years later,

Shanmughan Manjunath, an Indian Oil Corporation officer, was killed for shutting down a petrol pump that was selling contaminated fuel. The Whistle Blowers Protection Act, 2011, is an Act of the Indian Parliament that establishes a mechanism for investigating allegations of public servant corruption and abuse of power, as well as provides protection to anyone who exposes alleged wrongdoing in government bodies, projects, and offices. It's possible that the misconduct takes the form of fraud, corruption, or mismanagement. Fraud, corruption, or mismanagement are examples of misconduct. The Act was endorsed by the Indian Cabinet as part of a campaign to clean up the country's bureaucracy, and it was enacted by the Lok Sabha on December 27, 2011. When the Rajya Sabha approved the Bill on February 21, 2014, and the President gave his assent on May 9, 2014, it became an Act.

Corruption is a societal blight that obstructs healthy, balanced social and economic development. The lack of adequate protection for complainants reporting corruption, willful misuse of power, or willful misuse of discretion that causes demonstrable loss to the government or the commission of a criminal offence by a public servant is one of the impediments to eliminating corruption in the government and public sector undertakings. It was determined to pass a separate law to offer proper protection to those who expose corruption or wilful misuse of authority or discretion that causes the government to lose money, or who reveal the conduct of a criminal offence by a public official.Comparison of the 2015 Bill with the 2013 Amendments to the Whistle-blowers Protection Act of 2014. On February 21, 2014, Parliament enacted the Whistle-blowers Protection Act of 2014. On August 5, 2013, after the Bill was approved by the Lok Sabha, various modifications were circulated in the Rajya Sabha. However, when the Bill was enacted by the Rajya Sabha in 2014, these revisions were not included. On May 11, 2015, the Whistle-blowers Protection (Amendment) Bill, 2015 was tabled in the Lok Sabha. According to the Statement of Objects and Reasons, this Bill was submitted to give effect to prior revisions that were not passed. The provisions of the 2015 Bill are compared to those of the 2013 amendments in the table below. Despite opposition from the Opposition, the Lok Sabha (India's bicameral Parliament's lower chamber) enacted a Bill to alter the Whistleblowers Protection Act 2011 (passed by Parliament in 2014) on May 13, 2015. The Bill will now be presented to the Rajya Sabha for consideration (the upper house). It has been suggested that the Bill is being used to diminish the Act's effect. A public interest disclosure may be made before a competent authority by anyone, including a public official or an NGO, according to the Act. Regardless of the prohibitions of the Official Secrets Act of 1923, this would apply. Certain items were excluded from disclosure under Section 8 of the Act, including information likely to jeopardise India's sovereignty and integrity, the state's security, cordial relations with other nations, public order, decency, or morality, or information relating to contempt of court, defamation, or incitement to an offence. As may be the case with the revelation of the Cabinet of the Union Government or any of its committees' actions, as would be the case with the publication of the State Government's Cabinet or any of its committees' sessions. Other grounds for exempting material from disclosure are included in the amendment bill, including: Unless such information has been revealed to the complaint under the terms of the Right to Information Act, 2005, it relates to commercial confidence, trade secrets, or intellectual property, the revelation of which would undermine a third party's competitive position. Unless such information has been revealed to the complaint under the requirements of the Right to Information Act, 2005, information that is available to a person in his fiduciary function or connection; Information that might jeopardise a person's life or physical safety, or reveal the source of confidential information or assistance provided for law enforcement or security objectives;information that might obstruct the investigation, arrest, or prosecution of criminals. Unless such information has been revealed to the complaint under the requirements of the Right to Information Act, 2005, personal information that has no relevance to any public activity or interest, or that would constitute an unreasonable violation of the individual's privacy, It is believed that the amendment reduces the efficacy of the original Act by expanding the conditions in which information is not required to be provided. According to the Bill's Statement of Objects and Reasons, the 10 forbidden categories are modelled after those under the RTI Act of 2005. This analogy, however, may not be relevant. Unlike the RTI Act, the Bill requires disclosures to be made in confidence to a high-ranking constitutional or statutory authority. The RTI Act allows a public authority to reveal information if the public authority believes it is in the public interest; and (ii) a two-stage appeal process if information is not made available. Such clauses are not included in the bill. Despite the foregoing clarity, many employees are terrified of being victimised if they speak up. While companies may express a desire to be ethical and honest in their operations, you can only *"walk the talk"* if you support employees' freedom to express their concerns in a safe and open environment.

A competent body must recommend a banned disclosure to a government authority for final approval. The Bill, on the other hand, does not establish the requisite credentials or the process for appointing this authority. Other nations' whistle-blower laws similarly limit the sharing of certain types of information. These include national security and intelligence material obtained in a fiduciary role, as well as any disclosure expressly forbidden by law. It is critical for every firm to have clear communication throughout the organization and to set appropriate limits. Employees require a secure and private channel to express their concerns in the event of a problem. In this scenario, whistleblowing software is critical in providing employees with the opportunity to report wrongdoing.

You will come upon these ethical concerns in your business at some point. Even if you take all the essential safeguards, you should always be ready to deal with them. Use them as a learning experience in order to establish a stronger and more ethical business in this market. Organizations can learn from their errors, and the best way to do so is to communicate any issues to top management. If you have suspicions of criminal behaviour, have seen wrongdoing, or have ethical issues, you can express them anonymously by calling an anonymous whistleblowing hotline. While it is critical to speak out when you see unethical activity, the greater the dangers to the company or your direct management, the more pressure you may feel to go along with or overlook the behaviour, especially if blowing the whistle might jeopardise your career. Consider that, according to the 2016 National Business Ethics study conducted by the Ethics and Compliance Initiative and published by The New York Times, 53% of employees who reported ethical violations in their workplaces suffered some type of retribution. Using euphemisms to soften the gravity of unethical behaviour, delaying confronting the behaviour, or reasoning that most people would go along with the breach anyhow are all behaviours that may fester, driving off excellent employees, damaging careers, and putting the company in jeopardy.

Recent high-profile ethical issues, particularly those involving discrimination and sexual harassment, have shed focus on unethical workplace behaviour and how such failings may infect employee relationships, business policies, and operations. According to the Ethics & Compliance Initiative's 2018 Global Benchmark on Workplace Ethics, 30% of employees in the United States directly saw wrongdoing in the previous 12 months, a figure close to the global average for misbehaviour observation. These ethical infractions typically go undetected or unaddressed, and when they are coupled, they may cost a lot of money. Unethical business activities have caused more than half of the greatest bankruptcies in the last 30 years, including Enron, Lehman Brothers, and WorldCom, and can have a greater economic impact, estimated at $1.228 trillion in accordance with the Society for Human Resource Management.

Each is a significant example of corporate corruption, and the list is far from exhaustive. The list excludes undetected corruption, as well as scandals in government, education, healthcare, the military, money laundering, and tax evasion. It's worth reflecting on how difficult it is to maintain secrets these days. We live in a time when communication is instantaneous and inexpensive. Everyone has a camera-equipped cellphone. A flash drive may hold the equivalent of a file cabinet's worth of records. Corporate criminality would vanish without a strong mechanism to force employees to remain silent in the face of public scrutiny. Thousands of employees must be participating in corporate corruption. How can corruption continue when there are so many witnesses? Whistleblower retribution and blacklisting are the obvious solutions. Whistleblowers don't speak up because they are afraid of losing their jobs. Understanding the motives of employees is the first step in reducing corruption.

Whistleblowers' Safeguard

Why are average employees so deafeningly quiet? What is the mechanism that keeps people silent? Once you understand this, you may alter employee incentives such that similarly situated employees make different decisions in the future. You must also educate the public about the issue. There are several misunderstandings. The majority of individuals believe that corporate fraud and criminality are uncommon. They believe their boss does not and would not breach the law under any circumstances. Whistleblowers are viewed as troublemakers, or worse, and they believe corporate wrongdoing is unimportant. These findings are not supported by the facts. Yes, there are whistleblower protection laws and anti-retaliation procedures in place, but the public is well aware that whistleblowers are frequently punished and subjected to retaliation. Yes, there are whistleblower protection laws and anti-retaliation rules in place, but nonetheless, most people are aware that whistleblowers are frequently punished and retaliated against. As a result, they require a discreet, informal, unbiased, and independent resource to assist them in dealing with such difficulties. An ombudsman can help with that. Yes, there are whistleblower protection laws and anti-retaliation rules in place, but nonetheless, most people are aware that whistleblowers are frequently punished and retaliated against.

As a result, they require a discreet, informal, unbiased, and independent resource to assist them in dealing with such difficulties. An ombudsman can help with that.

Thousands of German car industry employees knew their employers were breaking the law in the years leading up to the VW diesel-gate incident, yet they all remained silent. Several of the world's major corporations were involved in a worldwide criminal conspiracy. Eleven million automobiles were sold worldwide with defeat devices, produced, and fitted. Over a five-year period, these vehicles accounted for 40% of VW's sales. It was a massive ruse. Because of the trickery, massive amounts of NOx, the substance that produces acid rain, were released into the environment. VW was fined $25 billion, Mercedes was fined 870 million euros, Porsche was fined $600 million, and BMW was fined $11 million. The system was clearly illegal, and a considerable number of employees were aware of it for more than five years.

Dieselgate and similar situations should serve as a wake-up call. We must understand that corruption, even by the world's most prestigious corporations, is a daily occurrence. It's past time to put a stop to this corruption, and there's a simple method to do so: promote whistleblowers. A hundred thousand fatalities may have been spared if Chinese officials had listened to coronavirus whistleblower Dr. Li Wenliang. The illicit emissions would have been stopped years sooner if any of the VW employees had gone to the press. Understanding why informed insiders remain silent about corruption, changing the rules of the game so insiders speak out, and ensuring regulators listen to and react correctly are the most effective paths to eliminating corporate wrongdoing. Corporate corruption is on the rise across the world. Audi, Barclays, Boeing, BMW, BP, CBS, Deloitte, Equifax, E&Y, FaceTime, Facebook, FoxxConn, FIFA, Fyre, J&J, Kobe Steel, KPMG, Nissan, Purdue, PWC, Rolls Royce, Samsung, Theranos, Turing Pharma, Mossack Fonseca, Uber, VW, Walmart, Wells, WeWork, Wirecard, and 1MBD are among the companies that Adelphia, AIG, Anderson, Banniter, Barclays, Bear, Deutsche, Enron, Global Crossing,

Healthsouth, HIH, Lehman, Madoff, Northrup, Olympus, Parmalat, Siemens, SocGen, Tyco, Waste Mgmt, UBS, and Worldcom join the classics: Adelphia, AIG, Anderson, Banniter, Barclays, Bear, Deutsche, Enron, Global Crossing, Wells, WeWork, Wirecard, and 1MBD are just some of them. As you read the list, your vision blurs.

Executives' Ethical Principles

- Ethical principles are ethical beliefs put into active language that provide norms or regulations specifying the types of conduct that an ethical person should or should not engage in. The features and ideals that most people connect with ethical behaviour are included in the following list of principles. Honesty In all of their transactions, ethical executives are honest and truthful, and they do not intentionally mislead or deceive people by misrepresentations, overstatements, partial truths, selective omissions, or any other method.
- Integrity ethical executives demonstrate personal integrity and courage of conviction by doing what they believe is right, even when it is difficult; they are principled, honorable, and upright, and they will fight for their beliefs. Trustworthiness Executives who act ethically are deserving of our trust. They are open and honest in providing pertinent information and correcting factual errors, and they make every reasonable effort to keep their pledges and obligations in letter and spirit. They do not use overly technical or legalistic interpretations of agreements in order to justify non-compliance or construct arguments for avoiding their obligations.
- Loyalty & ethical CEOs are trustworthy, demonstrating integrity and dedication to people and organizations via friendship in difficult times, support, and devotion to duty; they do not use or divulge confidential information for personal gain. They protect their capacity to make unbiased professional judgements by avoiding undue influence and conflicts of interest as much as possible. They are loyal to their employers and coworkers, and if they leave, they give appropriate notice, respect their former

employer's private information, and refuse to engage in any actions that take unfair advantage of their prior positions.

- Fairness in all transactions, ethical executives are fair and just. Fair people are committed to fairness, equitable treatment for all people, tolerance for and acceptance of variety, and they are open-minded; they are prepared to recognize when they are mistaken and, if necessary, adjust their stances and ideas. Ethical CEOs are loving, empathetic, benevolent, and kind, and they strive to achieve their corporate goals with the least amount of harm and the greatest amount of positive benefit.
- Ethical CEOs respect the human dignity, autonomy, privacy, rights, and interests of all those affected by their actions; they are courteous and treat everyone with equal respect and decency, regardless of gender, ethnicity, or country of origin. Observe the law. Ethical leaders follow the laws, rules, and regulations that govern their businesses. Excellence is a passion for me. Ethical executives strive for excellence in their work, are well-informed and prepared, and are always looking to improve their skills in all areas of responsibility.
- Leadership Ethical executives are aware of the responsibilities and opportunities that come with their position of leadership, and they strive to be positive ethical role models through their own actions and by assisting in the creation of an environment that values principled reasoning and ethical decision-making.
- Ethical executives strive to safeguard and enhance the company's good name and employee morale by engaging in no activity that may be seen as disrespectful to others and by taking whatever steps are necessary to address or avoid improper behaviour on the part of others.
- Accountability Executives who are ethical recognize and take personal responsibility for the ethical character of their actions and omissions in the eyes of themselves, their colleagues, their enterprises, and their communities.

Leadership Accountability

Although not all ethical infractions are as spectacular as those that grab headlines, all ethical violations are bad. When confronted with an unethical scenario or leader, consider what you value most as an individual and as a professional to help guide your reaction. Knowing whether to speak when might be a personal ethical quandary in and of itself. The *"Glassdoor"* effect when consumers believe internet reviews of their employers more than what firms convey and the trust impact when employee messages become viral on social media For the sake of the organization, companies must foster *"listen-up"* cultures by establishing internal reporting systems in which leadership and management listen to and encourage workers who speak out. This assures employees that their reports will be heard and taken seriously, and that things will be changed if required. Developing a culture of integrity and ethics in organizations as opposed to a an overreliance on laws and regulations. Finally, and most critically, every employee is watching for leadership accountability.

When firms undergo fast change of CEOs and other senior executives, it can be difficult to retain a consistent identity and set of values. It is vital to choose the proper people to head the company. If everyone in the organization lives the organization's ideals, promoting from within is one strategy to guarantee those values are preserved. However, this is not always practicable or feasible. When appointing senior executives, particularly CEOs, boards must examine individuals who are not just smart, but also have the chemistry, character, and moral competence to inspire and win the hearts and minds of all stakeholders. While continuous communication is crucial, firms should avoid repeating the same message since it can become stale, causing employees to overlook the underlying values and principles. To stay fresh, communicating values is similar to running a marketing campaign: it must attract people's attention and employ a variety of materials, forms, and communication channels. One technique to generate this level of attention is through the power of stories. Employees throughout the business feel at ease raising legal, compliance, and ethics issues and concerns without fear of reprisal. Senior leaders hold themselves and those reporting to them accountable for adhering to the law and organizational policy, as well as shared or organizational values.

Your organization sets a goal that looks improbable, if not unattainable (for example, a monthly sales figure or a product production number). While not intrinsically unethical. After all, having motivated leadership with ambitious corporate objectives is vital to innovation and success, the manner in which employees, and even some leaders, go about reaching the goal may raise an ethical red flag. Unrealistic goals can lead to leaders putting undue strain on their workforce, and employees may consider cutting shortcuts or breaching ethical or legal conventions to attain them. Cutting ethical corners is a shortcut that seldom pays off, and if your entire team or department is failing to reach goals, firm leadership requires that input in order to reassess those goals and re-evaluate performance.

Sexual Harassment

Whether in a developed, developing, or undeveloped country, sexual harassment in the workplace is a prevalent problem. Atrocities against women are endemic worldwide. It is a worldwide issue that has a detrimental influence on both men and women. It occurs more frequently in the female gender. No matter how hard one tries to protect, ban, prevent, or provide remedies, violations will always occur. As a result, women are subjected to a wide range of crimes, including female feticide, human trafficking, stalking, sexual abuse, sexual harassment, and the most horrific crime, rape. Harassment of a person (an applicant or an employee) because of their sex is illegal. Harassment can take many forms, including *"sexual harassment"* or unwanted sexual approaches, requests for sexual favours, and other forms of sexual verbal or physical harassment. Sexual harassment is unwanted sexual behaviour that causes a person to feel insulted, embarrassed, or intimated. Unwelcome The key word here is *"behaviour."* Unwelcome does not imply *"forced."* Even though the activity is rude and disagreeable, a victim may consent to it and actively participate in it. Whether the individual appreciated a date request, a sex-oriented remark, or both depends on all the circumstances. Sexual harassment is defined by the Supreme Court of India as any unwelcome sexually determined behaviour (whether directly or indirectly), such as physical contact and advances; sexually coloured remarks; showing pornography.The phrase *"unwelcome"* is a crucial aspect of the definition. Unwelcome or unwanted conduct or acts are strictly forbidden. Sexual or romantic involvement between consenting adults at work may offend bystanders or result in a breach of company policy, but it is not sexual harassment. Actual or attempted rape or sexual assault may be included. Whistling at someone is a bad idea. Smacking lips, wailing, and kissing noises Interacting with an employee's clothing, hair, or body in any way sexually touching or rubbing against another person. It's a prevalent misconception that sexual harassment in the workplace is restricted to exchanges between male bosses and female employees.

The Sexual Harassment of Women at Workplace (Prevention, Prohibition, and Redressal) Act was passed in 2013, defining sexual harassment and outlining the procedures for filing a complaint and conducting an investigation, as well as the actions that must be taken. The Kerala High Court on Thursday, March 17, 2022 ordered organizations affiliated with the film industry to make efforts to create a joint committee to deal with allegations of sexual harassment of women under the Sexual Harassment of Women at Workplace (Prevention, Prohibition, and Redressal) Act of 2013.

Sexual harassment can occur amongst coworkers for a variety of reasons, including the following:

- Harassment of a subordinate by a superior.
- Women are capable of sexually harassing men.
- Sexual harassment of both men and women.

Offenders might be bosses, coworkers, or non-employees such as clients, vendors, and suppliers.Everything has altered as a result of the #MeToo movement. Bill Cosby, Harvey Weinstein, Charlie

Rose, Kevin Spacey, Al Franken, Matt Lauer, Garrison Keillor, and other high-profile public personalities have urged institutions to take action through public forums and social media platforms. Victims of harassment have the ability to choose. They can either file an internal report and hope that their company responds appropriately, or they can choose to make their story public. In general, executives feel they understand and can define the culture of their organization. However, there may be a misalignment between management's concept of culture and how the rest of the business perceives it. It is a fallacy for executives to believe they always have their finger on the pulse of the organization's culture. Organizational values are a set of explicit principles that stress the organization's dedication to legal and regulatory compliance, honesty, and corporate ethics, among other things. Executive leadership and senior managers throughout the organization urge workers and business partners to conduct themselves legally and ethically, as well as in line with compliance and policy requirements. In doing so, the court emphasised that film production companies must follow the law against sexual harassment, also known as the POSH Act, which was approved by Parliament in 2013. Several Indian women took part in the #MeToo campaign.

Several women in India accused influential men of sexual harassment during the #MeToo movement, including actors, stand-up comedians, and senior journalists. The Supreme Court established the Vishaka rules in a 1997 ruling. This occurred in a lawsuit brought by women's rights organizations, one of which being Vishaka. They had launched a public interest lawsuit against Bhanwari Devi, a social worker from Rajasthan, who was allegedly gangraped. She had stopped the marriage of her one-year-old daughter in 1992, resulting in the claimed gangrape as a form of retaliation. The legally enforceable Visakha principles define sexual harassment and set three important tasks for institutions: prohibition, prevention, and reparation. The Supreme Court ordered that a Complaints Committee be established to investigate complaints of sexual harassment of women in the workplace.

In the last six years, the combination of a number of external variables has prompted businesses to treat sexual harassment in the workplace with the seriousness it deserves. Some businesses are going above and beyond the call of duty to find creative solutions to the problem of sexual harassment in the workplace. Nonetheless, numerous firms continue to underreport the number of such instances. However, the POSH Act has compelled businesses to follow its mission and make their workplaces safer for female workers. The increasing number of female employees in the workforce, greater diversity, the transition to a less formal work environment, and pervasive technology have all contributed to the necessary transformation. Various activities are used by various firms to monitor the pulse of their employees.

- Anonymous online surveys are conducted to find out if female employees are subjected to sexual harassment at work.
- Women-only interventions are advised to enable women to express their workplace harassment experiences.
- Men only interventions are carried out to ensure that male coworkers are aware of the true purpose of the act and do not feel threatened or excluded.
- To guarantee that staff cohesion is at its peak, joint interventions are used.
- Several external factors have combined to provide the necessary push to treat workplace sexual harassment seriously.

The media's enormous reach is assisting in giving sexual harassment the attention it has long deserved. Because of the power of social media, a single blog post by an employee alleging workplace harassment may bring his or her organization to its knees. In 2017, the Ministry of WCD introduced the "SHE-Box" (sexual harassment electronic box). This is an online complaint management system for female employees in the public and commercial sectors to document and resolve sexual harassment complaints. Lawyers are treating such matters seriously, and organizations such as the Sexual Harassment Law Compliance Advisory (SHLC) are helping businesses become POSH compliant by forming and training an ICC at their respective workplace. The International Labour Organization (ILO) established an international convention banning workplace harassment and violence on June 21, 2019. The worldwide effect of the # MeToo movement has added to the conversation about this treaty. The treaty specifically recognizes that gender-based violence and harassment, including sexual harassment, can adversely impede women's access to and continuing involvement in employment. National laws addressing workplace harassment, including sexual harassment, are required under the treaty. While there is no universal workplace violence and harassment legislation in India, the Sexual Harassment of Women at Workplace (Prevention, Prohibition, and Redressal) Act, 2013, was passed nearly six years ago with the goal of combating workplace sexual harassment.While India may be ahead in terms of legislation, the reality on the ground is quite different. According to surveys, while 38 percent of women have experienced or seen sexual harassment, 80 percent of occurrences go unreported. Sexual harassment is ubiquitous and detrimental across locations and sectors, notwithstanding the rise in reports following the # MeToo movement (due to increased awareness). Finally, the greater goal of national and international human rights frameworks in relation to sexual harassment can only be properly realised if survivors of sexual harassment are given the opportunity to seek remedy through an unbiased and devoted commission. Governments, as well as private players, have a responsibility to work toward this realisation and ensure harassment-free workplaces for everybody.

Racial And Gender Discrimination

The law requires organizations to be equal-opportunity employers. Organizations must recruit a diverse workforce, adopt regulations and training to encourage an equal opportunity program, and provide a welcoming environment for all types of people. Regrettably, many firms continue to flout statutory regulations. When employees are discriminated against or harassed because of their skin colour, ethnicity, gender, disability, or age, not only an ethical but also a legal barrier is crossed. Because most businesses are concerned about the costly legal and public repercussions of discrimination and harassment, you may encounter this ethical quandary in more subtle ways, ranging from seemingly harmless off-color comments by a boss to a more persistent group think mindset that can be harmful. This might be a group perspective toward another other group (for example, ladies aren't a good match for your group). Your best response is to maintain your own beliefs while opposing such intolerant, unethical, or illegal group norms by promoting an alternate, inclusive position as the best choice for the group and the organization. Harassment and discrimination are two of the most important ethical issues that business owners face today. If harassment or discrimination occurs in the workplace, the consequences might be disastrous for your company's finances and image.

Every business should be aware of anti-discrimination laws and regulations in place to protect employees from unfair treatment. The United States Equal Employment Opportunity Commission (EEOC) outlines numerous distinct forms of discrimination and harassment regulations that might affect your firm, including but not limited to:

- Age refers to anyone over the age of 40, as well as any ageist policy or treatment.
- Employees with physical or mental impairments are entitled to reasonable accommodation and equitable treatment.
- Equal pay is defined as equal pay for equal effort regardless of gender, ethnicity, religion, or other factors.
- Pregnant employees are given reasonable accommodations and equitable treatment.

- Employee treatment should be uniform regardless of race or ethnicity.
- Reasonable accommodations and equitable treatment are offered regardless of employee religion.
- Employee treatment should be uniform regardless of sex or gender identity.

Workplace Health and Safety

Employees have a right to safe working conditions as defined in the Occupational Safety and Health Administration's (OSHA) laws. According to their 2018 survey, 5,250 people in the United States died as a result of occupational accidents or illnesses at work. On average, this equates to more than 100 deaths every week, or more than 14 deaths per day. The top ten most commonly mentioned violations of 2018 were:Unprotected sides and edges, as well as leading edges, are examples of fall hazards. Hazard classification of hazardous compounds, for example, is an example of hazard communication. Scaffolding, for example, needs resistance and maximum weight figures. Emergency procedures and respiratory/ filter equipment requirements, for example, are examples of respiratory protection. Controlling hazardous energy, such as oil and gas, is an example of lockout/tagout. Powered industrial trucks, for example, fire truck safety standards. For ladders, for example, guidelines for how much weight a ladder can withstand. Methods of electrical wiring, such as how to wire a circuit to decrease electromagnetic interference, machine Guarding, for example, states that guillotine cutters, shears, power presses, and other machinery require point-of-operation guarding. For electrical general requirements, for example, do not place conductors or equipment in damp or moist areas. However, worries about health and safety should not be restricted to physical injury. In a 2019 study, the International Labour Organization (ILO) emphasised the growth of *"psychosocial hazards,"* as well as work-related stress and mental health problems. Job instability, excessive expectations, effort-reward imbalance, and limited autonomy have all been linked to health-related behavioural hazards such as sedentary lifestyles, heavy alcohol use, increased cigarette smoking, and eating disorders.

Compliance Management Approach

Ethics starts at home. A robust and well-communicated code of ethics, best articulated in terms of rules and procedures, is the cornerstone of an effective ethics and corporate compliance program. These rules and procedures establish the organization's culture and expected conduct for everyone who works in or with it. Being proactive also necessitates collaboration between the corporate compliance team and other departments and regulatory compliance groups in order to manage their compliance procedures, controls, templates, and schedules. This method provides the corporate compliance team with complete visibility into organizational compliance, allowing them to conduct regular or ad hoc evaluations to reduce infractions. The readiness of a business to deal with a compliance issue is crucial since it affects brand value and revenue. To that end, successful firms must be proactive in terms of developing controls and procedures, defining accountability, and centrally maintaining compliance requirements so that they are easily available to all departments involved.A risk-based approach to compliance and ethical management includes identifying and prioritizing high-risk areas inside the company, as well as prioritising, controlling, and monitoring such risks. Compliance risks may be assessed and graded from a variety of angles, including business unit, process, and geography. Organizations can efficiently arrange control testing based on the risk rating. Issues can alternatively be sorted by grade, effect, probability, or category. There is no way for a company to become compliant with laws and regulations overnight. Compliance is a continual process that necessitates organizations defining new goals, leveraging technology to achieve these goals, assessing the outcomes, and then working to improve the results by setting new targets. This ongoing process will aid in the integration of corporate compliance within the business.

Every regulated organization now needs a solid ethics and corporate compliance program. Organizations will not be able to completely comply with requirements if their personnel do not adhere to corporate policies and procedures. Investing in staff training is usually a wise decision. Employees must be aware of the organization's culture as well as its ethical limitations. Technology, in the form of learning or training management systems that make it simple to run and track different training programs, can play a key role here. Many firms have found it beneficial to offer hotline lines where workers may anonymously report concerns about bribery, fraud, ethical breaches, discrimination, and other workplace wrongdoing. Integrating hotlines with a company's corporate compliance program can be beneficial since it allows for the monitoring of each issue from inception to resolution.

When there are several subsidiaries scattered across different regions, policy design must take various elements into account, such as subsidiary location and industry. The key to policy development is to ensure that policies are relevant both internationally and locally. This contributes to ensuring that there are no gaps or loopholes in compliance. Automated technologies can add value by simplifying the policy management process. Every firm must have a compliance strategy in place to identify possible risks, develop strategies to minimize them in the short term, and create a long-term plan of action. These techniques must be extended to the departmental level, where compliance infractions and concerns may frequently jeopardise the organization's reputation. There must be programs, procedures, and technology in place to detect, prioritise, investigate, and resolve compliance infractions and threats before they become black swan occurrences. In order to mitigate these risks, strong regulations and practises are also required. In reality, having a strong corporate compliance program assists firms in staying in compliance with both external standards and internal rules and practises. Training personnel on policies can also help to ensure an ethical atmosphere. Building a good compliance and ethical program might be difficult at times.

A corporate compliance team's major role is to design compliance strategies and programs, as well as to implement procedures and tools to detect, supervise, and mitigate compliance concerns at the enterprise level.

Furthermore, as regulatory compliance requirements increase, the corporate compliance team must engagewith specific departments and regulatory teams to supervise compliance at the departmental level. A program like this not only ensures compliance with numerous standards, but it also assists organizations in proactively identifying risks, improving ethical behaviour inside the organization, and being audit ready.

Because of the COVID-19 epidemic, firms have been compelled to function with a geographically distributed staff. Employees are working involuntarily from faraway areas. Many people work in lonely, unmonitored, unpleasant environments that reduce attention and motivation. The never-ending Work From Anywhere (WFA) movement may have far-reaching unintended consequences for productivity, ethics, and compliance. While the COVID-19 epidemic hastened the trend toward working from anywhere, much more work needs to be done to address the ethics and compliance challenges that are prevalent in this new environment. While corporations and people have made significant fixed cost expenditures in transitioning from the office to remote working, the next steps need investments in technology, personnel training, and organizational structure changes to reduce the risks. Employees who have no ethical reservations about defrauding the government would almost never have any difficulty submitting claims against the company. During the COVID-19 outbreak, fraud has been extremely problematic. Because of present conditions, the possibility to get maximum benefits has arisen, and employees are opting to take advantage of it. As you can expect, this will not go unpunished, and these incidents should be reported. Taking anonymous action now will spare everyone from future troubles. The most difficult ethical challenge for any firm is to participate in any ethical battle at all. The pressures—both real and imagined—to maintain income, market footprint, and profitability almost always swamp out most decision-makers' capacity to give full priority to the practise of true ethical rigour on a daily basis. However, author believes the epidemic has had an influence on this sort of ethical dilemma among corporations. People have been focused on purchasing basic things since there has been a noticeable reduction in consumption. As a result, they ignored elements that were not essential. With this, there are inclinations for firms' advertising approaches to involve overpromising and misleading hopes in order to get customers to buy their goods. In times of crisis, it is unavoidable for enterprises to fight tooth and nail merely to stay in business.

During the epidemic, several firms relocated to remote locations and faced new to them ethical difficulties. Surveillance of their staff is one of the most prevalent methods. While many employers offer equipment for their employees, many others do not, and instead ask them to install monitoring software. As a business partner, it is critical to ensure that the limits are properly conveyed to workers in order to avoid misunderstandings and disputes surrounding employee privacy and free expression.

Dr. Amit Das, author and mentor discusses how accounting has always been at the forefront of ethical challenges in business. This form of wrongdoing appears to be inescapable and must be reported in all cases. Today, the number one problem in every company is ethics in accounting processes. They falsify their income and spending in order to qualify for tax breaks. They falsify their financial figures to appear more prosperous. Owners of businesses are now individually scrutinizing their documents to ensure their correctness. Accounting software applications are even used to help people manage and keep track of their finances. As companies fight to survive in the midst of the epidemic, they tend to exaggerate their reports in order to appear successful despite the circumstances. They expose themselves to legal implications for their ability to sustain their lives. As companies fight to survive in the midst of the epidemic, they tend to exaggerate their reports in order to appear successful despite the circumstances.

Organizations run by dishonest CEOs usually suffer from a toxic work culture. Leaders who take bribes, distort sales statistics and data, or press staff or business associates for favours whether personal or financial will belittle and intimidate their employees. With many companies now emphasising *"cultural fit,"* a toxic culture may be exacerbated by repeatedly repopulating the organization with like-minded individuals and harmful mentalities. Worse, hiring for *"cultural fit"* may be used as a pretext for discrimination, with extra ethical difficulties and legal ramifications.

The advancements in technology security capacity, which fall under the same umbrella as nondisclosure agreements, raise privacy issues for both clients and staff. Employers may now monitor employee activities on their laptops and other company-provided devices, and while electronic monitoring is intended to assure efficiency and production, it frequently borders on privacy invasion.

Growing Concern

- Many employers are concerned about current and former workers stealing information, especially customer data that is exploited by groups that compete directly with the firm. Corporate espionage occurs when intellectual property is stolen or confidential customer information is unlawfully disclosed. In order to deter these sorts of ethics infractions, companies may implement obligatory nondisclosure agreements with harsh financial penalties in the event of a violation.
- Every day, unethical behaviour and unlawful actions occur in the workplace, regardless of industry. Unethical behaviour has a negative impact on staff morale and corporate integrity. There are several instances of wrongdoing, ranging from fraud to discrimination to invasions of privacy. With the events of the COVID-19 epidemic, unethical behaviour in the workplace has also been on the increase. Author polled a group of business

executives to find out what the most frequent ethical problems are in today's firms.

- Having a personal disagreement with your supervisor is one thing, but reporting someone who is acting unethically is quite another. This can be shown in apparent ways, such as tampering with figures in a report or spending corporate funds on improper activities. It can, however, appear in subtle ways, including as bullying, receiving improper gifts from suppliers, or being asked to forgo a regular process only once. Abuse of leadership power is a sad fact, with research estimating that managers are responsible for 60% of workplace wrongdoing.
- Author discusses the necessity of environmental, social, and corporate governance, as well as how the COVID-19 epidemic has accelerated the demand for racial and gender equality. Common ethical problems encountered in corporations today include decisions or lack thereof about racial and gender equality, as well as the environment. Many businesses previously turned a blind eye to these difficulties, but this is no longer an option. Racial Equity Audit is now at the top of the priority list for many CEOs and boards of directors, as they see the impact it can have on their businesses. COVID-19 and social instability have intensified this demand since individuals have more time to focus and pay attention now that they are at home and online. Significant progress has been accomplished in recent history in terms of gender and race prejudice. New legislation and best practises have been put in place to reduce and prevent all types of prejudice. While prejudice still exists, there has been a significant improvement in recent years. Despite your progress, there are still far too many cases when incorrect judgments are made based on gender and ethnicity. Those who observe or are victims of such behaviour must be allowed to express their concerns without fear of reprisal. As a result, many firms are turning to technology to enable employees to speak up in a secure environment and contribute to a culture of integrity.

- Overpromising products or services to potential clients in order to make a contract has been a topic of discussion in the marketing business since the outbreak of the epidemic. During the marketing process, this ethical concern is a fairly prevalent inclination. Salespeople have a tendency to raise false hopes and exaggerate items or services without sharing the necessary information and method in order to complete a transaction. This ethical dilemma contradicts transparency, honesty, and the establishment of trust between the organization and its customers. It can also cause an information gap, which leads to poor business credibility. While it may seem appealing to engage in this sort of behaviour in order to keep your business afloat, it will end up doing more harm than good for all parties involved. Integrity is essential for any business's success and ultimately decides your capacity to sustain long-term connections with your clients.
- Laws and regulations have also been put in place to reduce ethical concerns about health and safety. The recent COVID-19 events have brought the significance of workplace health and cleanliness to the forefront. Increased usage of face masks, hand washing, and social isolation will likely reduce seasonal flu incidence in the future. The necessity for health and safety compliance is stronger than ever, and violations of these standards must be reported.
- While this may appear to be a small issue in the wider scheme of workplace ethics, inappropriate use of the internet and business technology costs organizations a substantial amount of time, worker productivity, and corporate revenue. According to one survey, 64% of employees visit non-work-related websites during the workday. It is a waste of not just business equipment and technology, but also company time. This *"little white lie"* of workplace ethics may be spreading, whether you're using hourly breaks to check your social media news feed or you're aware that a coworker is using corporate technological tools to work on freelance duties. When you're working.The answer is simple: if

you're working on the firm's computer on company time, don't do it, no matter how tempting it may seem. Slippery slopes are caused by ethical issues.

- According to a 2019 American Management Association poll, 66 percent of businesses monitor internet connections, 45 percent track content, keystrokes, and keyboard time, and 43 percent store and examine computer files as well as employee emails. Transparency is the key to employing technology monitoring ethically. According to the same poll, 84% of respondents polled According to the same report, 84 percent of those organizations inform their employees that their computer behaviour is being monitored. To avoid employee monitoring becoming an ethical problem for your company, both employees and employers should be aware of the real advantages of being observed, as well as whether it is a beneficial means of establishing a record of their job performance.

Building An Organizational Culture

The lessons from scandals and organizational crises dating back to the early 2000s are clear: firms are susceptible without an ethical and compliance culture. Culture is increasingly becoming a defined, measurable, and improved idea, rather than a lofty, fuzzy one. Strong cultures are defined by two characteristics: a high degree of agreement about what is valued and a high level of intensity about those values. In the long term, a strong culture of integrity serves as the foundation for a successful ethics and compliance program, which may provide a competitive advantage and serve as a significant organizational asset when properly integrated into a company.Organizations may face a variety of hurdles in building a strong culture of integrity and an ethics program, but there are solutions to overcome these challenges: Organizations may face a variety of hurdles in building a strong culture of integrity and an ethics program, but there are solutions to overcome these challenges:

- Organizations can use staff surveys and independent observers to build listening posts, such as cultural evaluations, to acquire a more accurate picture. While senior leadership may work hard to develop an integrity culture at headquarters, policies and communications might get lost in translation as one goes out of the central office. Culture must be actively and continuously addressed, especially in big enterprises with remote outposts.
- Employee turnover may also harm an organization's culture. Organizations now must appeal to the biggest multigenerational workforce in history. To build cultures that last, firms should promote an atmosphere that combines a *"something for everyone"* appeal with a set of consistent principles that all generations can accept. Internal disputes are resolved fairly at all levels of the company. Author observes that employees may not always agree with outcomes, but they are more likely to accept them if they think the process was properly handled.
- Cultural fit is one of the most difficult challenges in integrating a merged or acquired firm; in fact, it is one of the reasons such deals fail, despite the potential commercial benefits. As part of the due diligence process, executives may wish to undertake a cultural audit. If the values of the target firm differ greatly from those of the buyer, this might be a warning indicator. A well-thought-out integration strategy can assist both organizations in understanding and reinforcing desirable values.
- An organization is a group of individuals who share common interests and beliefs and work together to achieve a common objective. Creating a culture of integrity not only fortifies the business against risk, but it also fosters employee engagement and strong affiliations with all stakeholders.
- Nothing can wreak havoc on culture more than the naysayers. They can stymie the organization's operations by causing barriers. They should be recognized, coached, and given the opportunity to conform to anticipated conduct, or they should be removed from the organization.

- The business hires and screens people based on both character and skill. The onboarding process instils corporate values in new workers, and mentoring reflects those principles. When employees depart or retire, they are treated with dignity.
- The organization recognizes and promotes employees in part based on their commitment to ethical standards. It is obvious that good conduct is rewarded, but it is also evident that poor behaviour, such as attaining outcomes regardless of technique, may have negative effects.
- Operational directions and business imperatives are consistent with leadership messaging about ethics and compliance. Managers in the middle who hoist the banner: Front-line and mid-level managers put ideals into action. They frequently employ the power of stories and symbols to encourage ethical conduct.
- Many businesses are taking calculative steps to strengthen their code of conduct and related controls and processes, as well as to promote accountability for ethical behaviour through training and performance evaluations.
- Reward appropriate conduct while penalising inappropriate behaviour. Don't take sides. Leaders frequently fail to express their beliefs and expectations. More is preferable in this scenario.
- Conduct cultural evaluations to get to the heart of how individuals behave and think. Maintain a positive attitude in the middle: Much depends on middle management's ability to translate top-down tone into rules and procedures that drive day-to-day conduct.
- While many employees avoid discussing ethical issues for the reasons stated above, many others do so out of fear of reprisal. This may be solved by anonymous ethics reporting, in which anybody within a company can voice their ethical concerns while remaining accountable. A compliant workplace not only helps to recruit fresh talent, increase performance, and strengthen employee morale, but it also adds to a company's

overall success.

- Maintain interest Find new and imaginative ways to transmit cultural values and to recognize and reward values-based behaviour. To encourage people to relate their stories in order to bring their values to life.

After determining an organization's existing ethical situation, communicating the Code with workers, and developing an ethical position with visible top leadership buy-in, a targeted ethicalization process must be implemented through the following organization-wide practises:

- Using ethical hiring strategies in recruitment and selection means employing people who have strong ethical principles and emphasising ethics while hiring new personnel.
- Providing ethical training; emphasising the importance of strict adherence to the Code of Ethics; ensuring that the lessons learned are applied in the workplace; discussing ethical issues with new hires as part of their onboarding process; communicating core values to newcomers and others (core values serve as long-term guiding principles that must be repeatedly repeated through training, corporate videos, and public meetings to change behavior).
- Rewarding ethical behaviour; evaluating procedures as well as outcomes; avoiding a bottom-line mindset; measuring ethical behaviour; disciplining workers who break ethical norms.
- Raising Concerns and Protecting Whistleblowers by assisting employees in raising concerns when something goes wrong; creating an environment in which workers feel comfortable speaking up and addressing ethical concerns;Establishing a rigorous framework to protect the interests of whistleblowers.
- Holding workers responsible for their activities; accepting responsibility for one's own actions and effects.
- Taking ethical considerations into account when making decisions and discussing ethical issues at meetings.

However, important care must be taken here, and ethical hotspots in the organization must be addressed proactively. If this is not the case, decent people may do horrible things. Three significant organizational functions that put companies at risk are marketing, finance and accounting, and human resources. Several ethical derailers, such as skewed incentives, hyper-competitiveness, a weak accountability system, senior pressure, and so on, linger in these hotspots. Employees in such scenarios face ethical dilemmas as a result of the numerous facets of the issue. We live in a world where things aren't always black and white. Rather, it is tinted in various shades of grey. Situations are complicated, and having a variety of alternatives is the norm rather than the exception.In this environment, focusing on the ethical climate is critical because the ethical climate of an organization is the single source of a systematic strategy to establish and sustain a moral infrastructure that emphasises the relevance of ethical issues in everyday professional life.

An Ethical Dilemma

Ethical dilemmas, also known as ethical paradoxes in moral philosophy, are frequently evoked in an attempt to criticise or enhance an ethical theory or moral code in order to reconcile the contradiction. The necessity of ethical behaviour is emphasised by many organizations. An ethical dilemma is a circumstance in which a difficult decision must be made between two or more solutions, neither of which resolves the issue according to established ethical principles. When faced with an ethical quandary, a person must choose a path of conduct that contradicts an established code of ethics or societal norms, such as laws and religious teachings, or their own moral beliefs about right and evil.Workplace pressures, on the other hand, can occasionally drive employees to engage in dubious practises. This is due to the fact that ethical challenges occur in a variety of shades of grey, not just black and white. There's also the issue of managerial pressure to fulfil predetermined goals on a regular basis. Organizations specify the means to attain these goals, but what counts is the ultimate result, and the employee may face an ethical issue. Consider the situation of a new account executive who is still learning the ropes. He had been jobless for months when he was eventually hired, via the good offices of a senior business development manager at an FMCG company. Within months, the teenagers were confronted with an ethical problem. His donor continued to provide him with invoices for a few thousand dollars, instructing him to edit them. The trainee was torn between his honesty and his gratitude, and he didn't know what to do. Months later, the trainee told the head office's chief accountant of the problem. This information was subsequently relayed to upper management. Surprisingly, the upper brass found themselves in a Catch-22 predicament! The senior manager was bringing in millions of dollars every month in business. Sacrificing him to save a few thousand rupees didn't seem like a good idea. Nonetheless, it had an influence on the integrity of the organization. The problem was overcome by simply changing the rules. According to a circular, expense invoices may no longer be filed directly to accounts.These should instead be sent through the department leader. That put a stop to the 'adjustments' as well as the employee's and employer's ethical dilemmas.

When we think of ethical difficulties, we think of things like open fraud, embezzlement, shady transactions, nepotism, and so on. Without a doubt, there are incidents of clear-cut ethical infractions. In that circumstance, any Ethics Committee or HR Head's job might be eliminated. To deter unethical behaviour, most professionally operated businesses have established codes of conduct. The ground rules are spelled out at the time personnel are on boarded. The issue then becomes, How do you deal with such ethical dilemmas? There aren't any easy answers, to be sure. However, there are a few general principles to follow to help you negotiate such situations.

- It's common to throw problems under the rug in the hopes that everything will work out in the end. Unfortunately, it's possible that they won't. Remember that it only takes one lie to cover up a hundred. As a result, think about the consequences of reporting or not reporting the occurrence. Keep in mind that if anything goes wrong afterwards, you may have to deal with the consequences for the rest of your life. After evaluating these facts, take action.

- Putting off dealing with the problem won't help. It is preferable to figure out solutions to the problem as soon as possible. The longer the problem persists, the more difficult it becomes to resolve. It's also conceivable that the culprit is just putting himself out there. If you push back the first time, he or she is less likely to repeat the offence.
- If you're being ordered to do anything immoral, say something like, *"If I'm not incorrect, I believe the corporate regulations forbid such actions"*—or something similar. Questioning the allocation of such a duty will make the manager feel uneasy, and he or she may decide to cancel the request rather than risk others finding out.
- Suggest some other ways to do the task without violating business policies. Again, refusing to comply with an unethical request will make your boss apprehensive about asking you to do anything similar in the future.
- Consult with coworkers or friends who have more expertise and can better advise you on how to handle the problem. They could recommend a different course of action to address your ethical quandary. Finally, if none of the options above work, take matters into your own hands.

Regardless of the outcome, decide if you want to blow the whistle and then take a stand. When it's evident that you're not going to breach the rules no matter what, top leaders who are promoting unethical agendas will often back off. Most of you are confronted with so-called ethical quandaries in your daily lives, and it will be critical to investigate the methods and means of developing the moral fibre that will allow you to overcome the difficulties of Catch-22 scenarios. If you were to define an ethical dilemma, you could say that it is a complicated circumstance including an apparent conceptual conflict between moral imperatives, in which obeying one would result in transgressing the other.

Let's have a peek at your work environment. Employees are inclined to do personal business on company time since they spend so much of their daily hours at work. Setting up doctor's appointments on company phone lines, making vacation reservations using their employer's computers and Internet connections, or even making phone calls for a freelance side business, stock market transactions, social work as an office bearer, and other personal work such as job searches, interviews, and so on, all while on company time and using company resources are examples of this. This ethical quandary appears to be rather obvious at first glance. Conducting personal business on company time may be considered an abuse or, at the very least, improper. There are, however, shades of grey here. What if your spouse calls to inform you that one of your children is unwell or that there is an emergency? Is it okay if you make a doctor's appointment or if you respond to an emergency? A decent rule of thumb for an employee is to ask his boss or the company's human resources department for clarity on what constitutes an actionable violation and what is not. The current accepted standard as defined by the code of conduct or ethical code can also provide valuable knowledge, and employees can be sensitised appropriately.

Employees frequently hide their true feelings due to the demands of their jobs, family concerns, job instability, and so on. Some people even accept harassment, and some people don't bother reporting unpleasant things like conduct, wrongdoings, unethical activities, and corruption because they are afraid of losing their employment. They are afraid that if they report harassment, wrongdoings, or unethical acts by a superior, they will be considered troublemakers and will suffer as a result. The ideal method to handle this ethical problem is for HR professionals to produce the company's employee handbook, which covers all elements and the intended action by the workers, rather than just interacting with them on a regular basis and feeling their pulse.

In both text and spirit, the same must be followed. It is their responsibility to add clear wording that states that reporting harassing behaviour, wrongdoing, or non-compliance with corporate policy and standards will not result in retaliation. You can continue to discuss the ethical difficulties that we confront in your daily lives. The golden rule is that remedial action must be taken where there are conscious pricks. It's a good idea to have a look at this quote.

"Ethics isn't about platitudes, let alone tautologies, logic, or mathematics; it's about tough choices or dilemmas." Martin Cohen

A more comprehensive approach to today's significant ethical challenges in the technology sector may help organizations stand out, safeguard their reputations, and better plan for and protect the future. There is no denying that the IT business has been a huge success. Our digital civilization is powered by its omnipresent goods and services. However, the industry's long-term ubiquity, scope, and impact have pushed it to confront a slew of unexpected and challenging ethical challenges. These difficulties were not necessarily caused by the IT sector, but many in the industry have reached a *"convergence point"* where they can no longer ignore them.As a result of big tech's perceived influence, sluggish regulation, and a lack of consistent industry norms, many customers, investors, employees, and governments are demanding greater general accountability from businesses. In addition, the technology sector is becoming more self-aware, questioning its own ethical ideals and pondering how to properly control its growth and influence. It's commonly thought that the more power you have, the more responsibility you have to use it properly, regardless of who said it first. In an increasing number of sectors, the IT industry is being pushed to do more. Without a comprehensive approach to these challenges, IT businesses will be unable to address today's most pressing concerns while also failing to plan for tomorrow's. Technology businesses are being pushed to go above and above what is needed by law in terms of environmental sustainability. Some criticise the semiconductor industry for its energy use, inefficient supply chains, production waste, and water use in semiconductor manufacture. The good news is that technology firms have enough market clout to effect meaningful change. Tech corporations are among the world's greatest users of renewable energy, and they're seeking to power their vast data centres with it. Some projects are centred on reducing waste, increasing recycling, and promoting circular economy ideas. Examples include Cisco's Takeback and Reuse initiative and Microsoft's 2030 zero waste objective. Others, such as Amazon's Climate Pledge, strive for net-zero carbon emissions.Apple, for example, has committed to being carbon-neutral across all of its companies by 2030. Threats to the truth include disinformation, misinformation, deepfakes, and the weaponization of data, which are being used by hordes of people and groups to attack, manipulate, and influence for personal benefit or to sow havoc. Technology businesses have encouraged governments to create legislation that clearly defines duties and standards in order to help solve this intractable problem. They're also working more closely with law enforcement and intelligence agencies, making public reports on their discoveries and stepping up their overall vigilance and action. These challenges are inextricably linked, and relying on separate responses to each may no longer be sufficient. It's likely that a transition to a more comprehensive approach is required.

The advantages of using a comprehensive approach might be enormous. It might help minimize negative publicity, consumer reaction, and regulatory action, lessen environmental harm, avoid legal issues, and prevent societal fragilities from worsening. It's not only about avoiding negative consequences; it's also about producing favourable ones. According to the Deloitte Global 2021 Millennial and Generation Z Survey, over 70% of both millennials and Generation Z believe that corporations in general are more concerned with their own agendas than with the larger society. 20). Furthermore, just 47% of millennials believe business has a good influence on society. Finally, being able to demonstrate your ethical behaviour and offer examples to your clients may help you keep them.

Organizational Ethical Committee

Ethics and compliance are two distinct concepts that complement and strengthen one another. The battle against corruption is an important part of a company's ethics commitment. This commitment, however, must be backed up by precise rules and processes that will help the organization optimize its efforts to remove corruption from corporate activities. Third parties, elaborate montages, concealed conflicts of interest, and so on are all examples of corruption. It's crucial to specify exactly what behaviour is and isn't acceptable. Specific dangers should be addressed via the use of suitable measures and behaviour. Together, these procedures make up the company's anti-corruption compliance program, which allows it to demonstrate its commitment to ethical business practises. When backed up by a well-executed compliance program, stated pledges to ethics become meaningful. On the other hand, an anti-corruption compliance program by itself will not suffice. If a member of staff is hell-bent on evading anti-corruption compliance laws and procedures, he or she will find a way. There might be a variety of motivations: personal gain, a kickback from the bribe taker, or just an easier way to meet sales targets and earn incentives. Only a firm, clear stance on ethical business practises, along with a comprehensive program, can prevent an individual from acting corruptly. For greatest efficacy, ethics necessitates compliance processes, and compliance procedures necessitate ethics.

Only a firm, clear stance on ethical business practises, along with a comprehensive program, will prevent an individual from acting corruptly. It doesn't matter if the position is called *"Ethics Officer"* or *"Compliance Officer."* What matters is that the person assigned to this position understands that an anti-corruption compliance program must be backed by a strong desire to conduct business ethically and that ethical business practises are more effectively pursued when backed by a strong anti-corruption compliance program. Some businesses hire an Ethics & Compliance Officer, while others hire an Ethics Officer and a Compliance Officer, and still others hire a Business Compliance Officer and a Legal Compliance Officer. The company's decision to choose the path that best respects the company's history, organization, and core business is far more essential than the position's label. In difficult settings, compliance initiatives can provide a competitive edge. A good compliance program, on the other hand, needs a business culture that values integrity and ethical behaviour in order to maximise that advantage. It's worth noting that one of the most well-known American groups dedicated to this topic is called the *"Society for Corporate Ethics and Compliance,"* which emphasises that experts feel the two are inexorably linked, even though the issues and techniques of compliance and ethics differ.

Creating An OEC Desk

- Increase the number of in-person conversations to better understand difficulties.
- Invite individuals to tell the unvarnished truth; this aids in the dismantling of organizational silos.
- To discover and then root out hidden hazards, ask the correct questions of the right individuals.
- To get workers' attention, they published anonymised, sanitised examples.
- Communicate ethical guidelines in a unique way to ensure that they are imprinted on the mind for the rest of one's life.
- Make a positive first impression with HR during onboarding.
- OEC's internal branding includes an intranet, desktop branding, and a learning management system (LMS).
- Obtain the CEO's and upper management's support. To avoid compliance fatigue, send reminders on a frequent basis.
- To minimise training weariness, create a calendar for a yearly multiple training program and make sure you're making the most of your learners' time.

- To make OEC intervention more meaningful and effective, use risk or role-based training.
- Through a mobile application, they promote microlearning, bite-size learning, and burst learning methods.
- Develop local trainers, such as managers, for a long-term training program.
- Inform your employees about cyber security and the dangers of social media.
- Hire a third-party study team to evaluate the existing situation or operational flaws.
- Appoint a third-party audit to eliminate any potential prejudice.
- Emphasize the necessity of anonymous reporting in order to avoid future business risks.
- Create a hotline to swiftly obtain first-hand information.
- Creating a dashboard for current procedures and a report on their progress to share with the CEO
- Reduce your COBC certification procedure and encourage all staff to participate in quarterly certifications.
- Create a document library and an online bank of all sorts of SR applications and forms for Ethics and Compliance.
- Real-time regulatory needs should be reflected in policy.
- It is necessary to guarantee that concerns about ethics and compliance are properly examined, monitored, handled, and addressed.
- Ascertain that programs for measuring efficiency and identifying possible areas for improvement are in place.

Existing Challenges

Ethical difficulties in a company may be a challenging challenge for any business owner to handle. Though there are rules and legislation in place to hold employees and employers accountable, they do not completely prohibit people from acting unethically. According to the 2019 Global Business Ethics Survey, 25% of employees believe that their top managers do not grasp critical ethical and regulatory business risks throughout the corporation.

Ethical concerns in business cover a wide range of topics that fall under the purview of an organization's ethical standards. Fundamental ethical challenges in business include supporting honesty and trust-based behaviour, but more sophisticated issues include accommodating diversity, empathic decision-making, and compliance and governance that is compatible with the organization's fundamental principles. According to the 2019 Global Business Ethics Survey, 25% of employees still believe that their top managers lack integrity. Long-held views that have been shown to be effective in the past may need to be altered. With a more ethical approach, there will likely be greater dialogue and transparency regarding the trade-offs between efficiency and performance.

- It is critical to find skilled ethical specialists who can advise the business while also understanding human behavior, prejudice, and unanticipated consequences.
- Existing corporate structures may have difficulties retaining both cash streams and good ethical principles.
- It's possible that a thorough ethical strategy may be more costly. It may take longer to design software and products that are fully aware of the true consequences.
- Engineering procedures may need to be altered.
- It may be necessary to establish new methods for evaluating, recognising, and rewarding executives, employees, and project teams.

Technology Businesses should no longer be focused only on growth and be competent at business. They should think about the ethical implications of their actions in a systematic way to better navigate the grey zones and avoid unintended effects in the future. Finally, it's not only about developing ethical and trustworthy technology; it's also about making it easier for the entire sector to make ethical and trustworthy judgments. Taking a comprehensive approach to the sector's ethical challenges and fostering foresight and a systems perspective will help assure a more sustainable industry and foster long-term trust with consumers, partners, employees, governments, and the general public. This is true not only for today's problems, but also for those that will inevitably arise in the future. Examine instances of ethical dilemmas to learn how you could approach these challenging circumstances. Managers are put to the test in the workplace when faced with the task of addressing an ethical problem. Certain instances frequently fall outside of the scope of processes or the formal code of conduct, putting managers under pressure. The challenge with ethical decision-making is that no one option can be made in isolation; each decision has an impact on a number of others, and the goal is to strike a balance to arrive at a win-win situation. Though there are no hard and fast rules for resolving ethical concerns, managers can take a number of steps to do so. Because of the growing use of social media, employees' online behaviour has become a determinant in their job status. The ethics of terminating or disciplining employees for their internet postings is a tricky issue. However, when an employee's online activity is taken into account, a boundary is frequently drawn.

However, when an employee's online activity is seen to be disloyal to their company, a boundary is frequently drawn. This implies that a Facebook post complaining about work is not unlawful in and of itself, but it can be punished if it causes a decrease in business. Similarly, business owners must be able to appreciate and not penalise employees who act as whistleblowers to regulatory authorities or on social media. This means that workers should be encouraged to raise awareness of workplace breaches online rather than penalised for doing so. Any firm must follow proper bookkeeping procedures. "Cooking the books" and other unethical accounting practises are severe concerns for firms, particularly publicly listed companies.

Compliance Startegy

To manage ethical concerns in business that occur in your firm, you must first have a complete awareness of what those difficulties might entail. Understanding how to recognize and, more importantly, prevent these issues from becoming a problem will help you keep your emphasis on business development and success rather than correction. There is no one-size-fits-all solution for businesses when they begin to establish a comprehensive strategy. These challenges can be daunting when they are considered as a whole, and there is no obvious road ahead. It will very certainly need a commitment to numerous orthodoxies throughout an organization's culture, financial plans, and operational procedures, as well as a willingness to confront them.

- There are three key ideas in ethical decision-making that may be applied to solve problems. These are the three principles of intuitionism, moral idealism, and utilitarianism.
- The intuition principle operates on the idea that the HR person or management is knowledgeable enough to see the gravity of the issue and act appropriately, so that the final choice does not cause harm to any individual concerned, directly or indirectly.
- The principle of moral idealism, on the other hand, maintains that there is a clear contrast between what is good and what is terrible, and that this is true in all cases.
- Moral decisions must be considered before being made, rather than being taken at face value. It's a great idea to make up hypothetical situations, create case studies, and then engage others in brainstorming on the same. This sheds some light on previously undisclosed issues and broadens the scope of comprehension and logical decision-making.
- The management uses the balance sheet technique to lay out the benefits and drawbacks of the decision. This aids in gaining a clearer view of things and better arranging them.
- One useful approach is to state one's position on various ethical concerns clearly and send a clear message to all members of the organization, especially those who are more vulnerable to unethical actions. As a result, employees will be less likely to use unethical methods as a result of this.

- Integrating Moral Decision-Making and Developing a Strategic Management Plan. Morality and ethics are frequently discussed issues, and ethical perfection is practically impossible to acquire.
- Integrating ethical decision-making into organizational strategic management is a better strategy to cope with this. The method by which the HR manager obtains a viewpoint that differs from the typical employee- or stakeholder-oriented viewpoint.

Taking a comprehensive approach to ethical challenges, if done well, may promote market distinction and disruption. The strategy might be used to better recruit and retain new generations of talent. You might be able to retain more consumers if you increase your customer retention.Admitting that your firm has an *"ethics issue"* may be the first hurdle to overcome. In a poll of technology professionals conducted by Deloitte, 82 percent strongly believed that their organization was ethical. Only 24% strongly agreed that the IT industry has an ethical approach to the goods and services it develops. At present, taking a comprehensive approach to ethical challenges may appear to be someone else's concern.

Summing Up

An organizational Ombudsman gives opportunities for people with problems to bring their complaints forward securely and effectively. Ombudsperson is a source of new issue discovery and early warning, as well as systemic reform ideas to enhance existing systems. Most people are aware that whistleblowers are frequently punished and retaliated against. Ethical executives strive to safeguard and enhance the company's good name and employee morale by engaging in no activity that may be seen as disrespectful to others. Developing a culture of integrity and ethics in organizations is one strategy to guarantee those values are preserved. Sexual harassment is unwanted sexual behaviour that causes a person to feel insulted, embarrassed, or intimated management system for female employees in the public and commercial sectors to document and resolve sexual harassment complaints. Every regulated organization now needs a solid ethics and corporate compliance program. The readiness of a business to deal with a compliance issue is crucial since it affects brand value and revenue. Being proactive also necessitates collaboration between the corporate compliance team and other departments and regulatory compliance groups. During the COVID-19 outbreak, fraud has been extremely problematic. People have been focused on purchasing basic things since there has been a noticeable reduction in consumption.

With the events of the COVID-19, unethical behaviour in the workplace has increased. Author polled a group of business executives to find out what the most frequent ethical problems are in today's firms. Strong cultures are defined by a high degree of agreement about what is valued and a high level of intensity about those values. Naysayers can stymie the organization's operations by causing barriers. Good conduct is rewarded, but it is also evident that poor behaviour may have negative effects. When faced with an ethical quandary, a person must choose a path of conduct that contradicts an established code of ethics.

A more comprehensive approach to today's significant ethical challenges in the technology sector may help organizations safeguard their reputations and better plan for and protect the future. Ethical concerns in business cover a wide range of topics that fall under the purview of an organization's ethical standards. There are no hard and fast rules for resolving ethical concerns, but managers can take a number of steps to do so. There is no one-size-fits-all solution for businesses when they begin to establish a comprehensive strategy. Integrating ethical decision-making into organizational strategic management is a better strategy to cope with this. The strategy might be used to better recruit and retain new generations of talent.

CHAPTER SIX

CONCLUSION

Make Your Ethical Roadmap Ready

"A 'no' uttered from deepest conviction is better and greater than a 'yes' merely uttered to please, or what is worse, to avoid trouble." – and "You must be the change you wish to see in the world." – Mahatma Gandhi

There are various everyday steps you can take to successfully detect and, more significantly, discourage ethical concerns in business from developing in your firm. When making decisions, be sure to express and enforce a strong code of ethics, and expect your workers to do the same. Maintain an awareness of the anti-discrimination legislation in your area. Keep up-to-date on the rules that affect your business, and make sure your organization is following them. Work with accountants to ensure that your financial reports are transparent and honest. Be present in your organization, ensuring that your organization and its people are constantly doing the correct and ethical thing.

Creating a company culture in which workers feel safe raising their voices about everything from sexual harassment to sentiments of being insulted is a clear message for firms and ethics and compliance authorities. This allows your compliance programme to address concerns before they become scandals, preserving the integrity of your organization's culture internally and its reputation internationally. And never, ever accept retribution.

Poor corporate governance can lead to conflicts of interest, expropriation, and discrimination against minority shareholders. Small shareholders with little effect on the stock price are swept aside to create room for the interests of majority shareholders and the executive board. It has the potential to undermine public trust and taint society as a whole.

A lack of corporate governance may result in economic loss, corruption, and a damaged image, not only for the company, but for society as a whole, or even worse, for the entire world. This type of corporate governance is also intended to reduce risk and eliminate corrosive components inside a company. Corporate governance makes businesses more responsible and transparent to investors, and it equips them with the tools they need to address genuine stakeholder concerns, including long-term environmental and social development. Increased access to finance promotes new investments, boosts economic growth, and creates job possibilities, all of which contribute to development.

Avoiding ethical concerns in a company always begins at the top. Transparency and ethical company practises may be ensured by providing clearly established policies and processes that guarantee such policies are both acknowledged and adhered to.

As previously established, ethics and compliance are inextricably linked. In general, compliance is more effective in lowering risks when there is a strong ethical culture in place, and in the absence of a compliance programme, those who actively strive to violate laws and norms of behaviour can cause chaos. Strong cultures are defined by two factors: a high degree of agreement on what is valued and a high level of fervour about those values.

In the end, what happens to the top achievers who break the rules sends the most powerful message to the organization. Whistleblowers will get a new voice as regulatory scrutiny grows, and the voice of the whistleblower grows stronger as well. Before going public, corporations must listen to and resolve the concerns of whistleblowers. Managing culture and free speech in the workplace amid polarising times continues to focus on race, gender, sex, sexual orientation, gender identity, national origin, and religion—as well as people's rights to fair treatment, protection, and the rights and benefits of other. As privacy rules and the settings they govern develop, chief compliance officers are becoming increasingly concerned about data privacy. It is necessary to provide a safe and courteous workplace. As traditional networking models give way to online networks that provide new and unprecedented opportunities to exchange ideas and interact, the role of the compliance professional evolves and innovates.

Suggestions

Ways to Improve Your Workplace Ethics and Compliance

" It takes 20 years to build a reputation and five minutes to ruin it. If you think about, you'll do things differently."- Wareen Buffett

From a large accounting fraud case in Germany to deceptive consumer techniques among Chinese-based corporations to unethical environmental activities in the United States, there is a long list of ethics and compliance failures in the business world. Your company's excellent name and stakeholder trust are two of its most valuable assets. By fostering an environment in which ethical behaviour is the standard, you can safeguard your company's reputation while also increasing employee engagement. Take the following methods to reduce your ethical risk:

- Assess your requirements and resources honestly.
- Create a solid foundation.
- Create an integrity-driven culture from the top down.
- Maintain a "values focus" in all situations, big and small.
- As required, re-evaluate and revise.

A good strategy is the foundation of any successful business. So, too, do effective ethics and compliance initiatives. To design a relevant and meaningful plan, you must first understand the terrain. Your program can only be effective if you start with an accurate assessment of your current strengths and areas of weakness. Your internal efforts should begin with risk assessment, followed by gap analysis and program evaluation. Audit reports are also an important component of the puzzle.

Your internal assessment to comprehend the situation on the ground:

- It is critical to understand that what ethical issues arise frequently in our work?
- Where are our most vulnerable points?
- Which ethical and compliance materials will be most beneficial to employees?
- What kind of assistance is most likely to be used and beneficial?
- What groups' input is needed for the development of our code and values?
- Which personnel groups, locations, business divisions, and so on constitute possible hot spots?
- What are the values that our organization and its workers hold dear?
- What values are required for our business, and particularly for our work?
- Who may be of assistance?

There are several methods for gathering information. Focus groups give a deep, rich picture of the status of ethics in your company by allowing a representative sampling of the greater community to express their ideas and experiences. Surveys (internal or done by a third party) allow you to collect information from a much broader group of your workers, compare findings, and analyze data by relevant subgroups (staff levels, departments, and units, for example). Start with ethical leadership at all levels of management if you're looking for a solution to the recurring challenge of how to foster an environment of trust, responsibility, and respect in the workplace.

Once you've identified your needs, you can put the tools in place to solve them by developing a strong ethics and compliance program. The good news is that such a program has an impact. The Ethics Research Center (ERC), the research arm of ECI, demonstrated as part of the 2011 National Business Ethics Survey that an ethics and compliance program is a powerful tool for reducing pressure to compromise standards and observations of misconduct; increasing employee reporting of observed misconduct; and decreasing retaliation against whistleblowers. In short, when a corporation invests in ethics, it makes a difference. Fewer employees feel pushed to breach the rules, and fewer wrongdoings occur. When improper behaviour occurs, employees notify management so the problem can be addressed internally.

COVID has struck you like a tsunami, putting your business partners and staff in a state of anxiety. Employees need to know that they can trust management to be honest and straightforward with them today more than ever before, since ambiguity breeds worry and dread. It's also a chance to develop a strong ethical culture that may support a business's future survival since employees will be glad to work for a firm that cares about them and has their back. These feelings must not be suppressed or disregarded, but rather recognizesd in order to create a secure environment. If properly implemented, staff will go above and beyond the call of duty to guarantee that you all get through this together.

Organizations now operate in such a dynamic and competitive environment that you must adapt on a regular basis. Most change programs, on the other hand, fail to provide the desired results, and people's attitudes are a major contributor. Some people may welcome change because they see it as an opportunity to gain advantages and advance in the company; others, on the other hand, see it as a risk and have negative attitudes toward it. In the latter case, people are thought to be resistant to change. This resistance might be due to their inability to adapt their behaviour, abilities, or dedication in order to fulfil the new standards; they may lack skills associated with change preparedness. People have a natural urge to fit in and adhere to the conventions of those around them, even after they have graduated from high school. Although it may be difficult to acknowledge, most people's ethical standards are very adaptable. Although most individuals want to *"do the right thing,"* the idea of the right is often impacted by who they associate with. Culture is important.

Fortunately, a strong ethical culture is significantly more likely to develop if your firm has painstakingly created an ethics and compliance program and integrated it into the everyday operations of the corporation. According to research, a good ethics and compliance program contributes to the development of a culture of integrity in which everyone *"walks the talk."* Employees at all levels are dedicated to doing what is right and respecting principles and standards in an organization with a strong ethical culture.

Quality procedures must be championed throughout business, with leaders benchmarking successful firms, implementing quality innovations, and establishing standards and measures in every area. Your ethics and compliance program must be a fundamental, integrated component of your job and the way you do it, ensuring that workers understand how to respect ethical and compliance standards in their work and feel supported in their efforts. Maintain established rules for ethical workplace behaviour as well as standardized training that provides information on ethical and compliance issues. A successful ethical and compliance programme will include the following characteristics:

- The ability to criticize management without fear of repercussions.
- Rewards for adhering to ethical norms.
- Not incentivizing questionable behavior, even if it is illegal.
- Not encouraging problematic behaviors, even if they are beneficial to the organization.
- Positive feedback for ethical behaviour.
- Employee preparation to handle wrongdoing and employees' openness to seeking ethics guidance.
- A method for reporting possible infractions in confidence or anonymously.
- Conduct performance assessments.
- Discipline systems for offenders discuss the significance of ethics.
- Keep employees up-to-date on problems that affect them.
- Keep pledges and obligations made to employees and stakeholders.

- Praise and recognize ethical behaviour.
- Hold people who break norms, particularly leaders, responsible.
- Exhibit ethical behaviour both professionally and individually.

Leaders are key corporate culture drivers; they set the tone in every firm. They select who gets seen, who gets promoted, and what deserves to be rewarded and recognised. They are the standard bearers. They serve as an example. Several actions should be taken by leaders to foster a strong moral culture. Character is everything. Ethical leaders demonstrate integrity not just in their professional lives, but also in their personal relationships. In an age of social media, private conduct frequently becomes public information, affecting employees‘ perceptions of the kind of people their bosses are. While senior executives establish the tone for the business as a whole, supervisors influence the day-to-day conditions in which people work and make choices. Supervisors' behaviour has a significant influence on employees‘ and their working behaviour. When a crisis occurs, leaders should realise not just the ethical dimension of the situation, but also the teachable moment it represents. Because of the depth of emotion involved, Edgar Schein, the pioneer of the study of corporate culture, observed that periods of crisis are particularly strong culture-builders. Employees learn a lot about their leaders' objectives and character when they display their true colors. Employees learn that ethics matter when leaders make values their touchstone in times of distress.

Ethics is about making decisions, both major and minor. Organizations with integrity maintain their ideals front and centre in both commonplace and exceptional situations. Corporate values should be included and expressed in a variety of procedures that drive the company's day-to-day operations, including:

- Human resource policies and their implementation.
- A system of rewards.
- Hiring and retaining employees.

- Management and assessment of performance.
- Decisions on promotions.

Situations and needs will shift. You must understand what is working, what isn't, what new vulnerabilities have appeared, how far you've come, and where there is still work to be done. Maintain a rigorous approach to reviewing the condition of ethics and compliance in your organization on a frequent basis. Risk assessments, follow-up surveys, and regular or continuous focus groups will help you keep your program relevant while minimising risk. Regular assessments will also demonstrate internally that the resources you've invested in ethics and compliance have made an impact.

References

- The Remix, How to Lead and Succeed in the Multigenrational Workplace by Lindsey Pollak, 2019
- The Ethics Of Money Production by Jorg Guido Hulsmann, 2018
- Business Ethics, The Search for Elusive Idea by Todd Pheifer, 2017
- Unleashing Capacity, The Hiddeen Human Resources by Rita Trehan, 2016
- Business Ethics, An Ethical Decision –Making Approach by Mark S Schwartz, 2017
- Ayn Rand and Business Ethics by Stephen Hicks, 2019
- A Good Life In The Market by Gary Chartier, 2019
- Business Ethics, Faith That Works by Larry Ruddell, 2014
- Global Business Ethics by Ronald Francis, 2015
- Bad Pharma How drug companies mislead doctors and harm patients, 2014
- Conscious Leadership by John Mackey, Steve Mcintosh, Carter Phipps, 2020
- Business Ethics lessoned Learned by Richard m Bowen, Niki Nicastro McCuistion, 2017
- Ethics For Managers by Joseph Gilbert, 2016
- Believe in People by Charles G Koch, Brian Hooks, 2020
- Business Ethics by Stephen M Byars, Kurt Stanberry, 2018
- Business Ethics Case Studdies and Selected Readings by Marianne M Jennings, 2017
- Business Law, The Ethical, Global,and E-Commerce Environment by Arien Langvardt, A james Barnes, Jamie darin Prenkert, Martin A McCrory, 2018
- Ethics in Information Technology, George Reynolds, 2018
- Law and Ethics In The Business Environment by Terry Halbert, Elaine Ingulli, 2017
- Business Ethics Mindtap management by O C Fereel, John

Fraedrich, Ferrell, 2018

- Business Ethics best practices for Designing and Managing Ethical Organizations by Denis Collins, 2018
- Business Ethics Managing Corporate Citizenship and Sustainability in the Age of Globalization by Andrew Crane, Dirk Matten, Sarah Glozer, Laura Spence, 2019
- The Power Of And, Responsible Business Without Trade-Offs by R Edward Freeman, Bidhan l Parmar, Kirsten Martin, 2020
- Resisting Corporate Corruption by Stephen v Arbogast, 2017
- Markets, ethics, and Business Ethics by Steven Scalet, 2018
- Managing Business Ethics by Linda K Trevino, 2017
- Business Ethics For Better Behavior by Jason Brennan, William English, John Hasnas, Jaworski, 2021
- Business Ethics In Action by Domenec Mele, 2019
- Organizational Ethics by Craig E. Johnson, 2021
- Managing Business Ethics by Alfred A Marcus, Timothy J Hargrave, 2020
- Business Ethics by William H Shaw, 2016
- Business Ethics Decision Making for Personal Integrity & Social Responsibility by Laura Hartman, Joseph DesJardins, Chris MacDonald, 2020
- Business Ethics Moral Principles That Govern the Conduct of Businesses by Razaq Adekunle, 2020
- This is Business Ethics by Tobey Scharding, 2018
- Social Entrepreneurship and Business Ethics Understanding the Contribution and Normative Ambivalence of Purpose-driven Venturing by Anica Zeyen, Markus Beckmann, 2018
- The Rise Of Business Ethics by Bernard Mees, 2019
- Issues in Business Ethics and Corporate Social Responsibility by Sage Researchers, 2020
- Business Ethics A Philosophical and Behavioral Approach by Christian A Conrad, Denica Webb, 2019
- Strategy, Law and Etyhics for Business Decisions by Christine Ladwig, George Siedel, 2020
- Business Ethics Now by Andrew Ghillyer, 2017

- Corporate Social Responsibility by Andreas Rasche, Mette Morsing, Jeremy Moon, 2017
- Business Ethics by Alejo Jose G Sison, 2018
- Understanding Business Ethics by Peter A Stanwick, Sarah D Stanwick, 2015
- A contemporary Look at Business Ethics by Ronald R Sims, 2017
- Business Sustainability, Corporate Governance, and Organizational Ethics by Zabihollah Rezaee, Timothy Fogarty, 2019
- The Business Guide to Effective Compliance and Ethics Why Compliance isn't Working - and How to Fix it by Andrew Hayward, Tony Osborn, Thomas Hickey, 2019
- Business Ethics, Contemporary Issues and Cases by Richard A Spinello, 2019
- Business and Professional Ethics by Leonard J Brooks, Paul Dunn, 2020
- Intentional Integrity: How Smart Companies Can Lead an Ethical Revolution by Robert Chestnut, 2020
- Governance, Risk Management & Compliance by Richard Steinberg, 2020
- The Business Guide to Effective Compliance & Ethics by Hayward & Osborn, 2020
- The Business Guide to Effective Compliance and Ethics: Why Compliance isn't Working - and How to Fix it by Andrew Hayward and Tony Osborn, 2019
- Corporate Risks and Leadership: What Every Executive Should Know About Risks, Ethics, Compliance, and Human Resources by Eduardo Esteban Mariscotti, 2021

About The Author

Dr. Amit is the founder of Accumentor, a consultancy firm set up by him in the human resource solution space, which is focused on developing processes for people. It offers consultancy in learning management, mentorship, performance coaching, training and development, psychometric analysis, HR processes and interventions. He was formerly the Director of Expertell Learning Point.

Dr. Amit Das is an experienced sales, training, and learning professional with more than 20 years of working history in the healthcare, medical devices, and learning management industries. Dr. Amit is a seasoned training professional with rich experience and a successful track record in aligning learning and training solutions to key business strategy with a strong focus on flawless execution excellence to facilitate individual, business divisional, and organizational performance. He keeps relentless focus on measuring training impact and ROI, people capability building graphs, training process governance, performance coaching, and strategic thinking. These have been some of his key individual success traits. His core capabilities include performance coaching, designing training and development frameworks and facilitation of technical skill building, psychometric assessment and analysis, competency framework development and assessments, content design and facilitation of soft skills and leadership programs, E-Learning Platform development, Learning Management Systems, Learning Impact Measurement, Talent Analysis and Performance Management System Review, Performance Coaching and Counselling.

His interests are in the areas of leadership development, coaching competency, mentorship, and motivational complexities related to organizational issues. His hobbies include public speaking, content creation, and reading books.

He has a Ph.D. and a Fellowship in strategic learning, along with his first class degrees in Human Resource Management and Corporate Laws from the top business schools in India. He is a certified professional coach from U.K. and behavioral coach from U.S.A.

www.ingramcontent.com/pod-product-compliance
Ingram Content Group UK Ltd.
Pitfield, Milton Keynes, MK11 3LW, UK
UKHW042019190726
13854UKWH00005B/2373